HE NEVER STOPS WORKING

A Story that Reveals God's
Unfailing Love and
Faithfulness

Amy J. Malay
&
Jebastin J. Malay

HE NEVER STOPS WORKING

A STORY THAT REVEALS GOD'S UNFAILING LOVE AND FAITHFULNESS

Amy J. Malay & Jebastin J. Malay

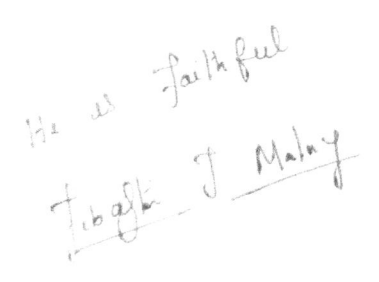

And I am certain that God, who began a good work within you, will continue his work until it is finally finished on the day when Christ Jesus returns. Philippians 1:6 NLT

Copyright © 2020 Amy J. Malay & Jebastin J. Malay

All rights reserved. This book or any portion thereof may not be reproduced or used in any manner whatsoever without the express written permission of the publisher, except for the use of brief quotations in a book review.

ISBN: 9798625313940 (paperback)

Cover image and design by:
Blessed Man Branding Services

Manuscript design by: Amy J. Malay

Printed by:
Kindle Direct Publishing in the United States of America

First printing, 2020.

Self-published by:
Amy J. Malay
1002 Union School Road
Mount Joy, PA 17552

www.johnmaxwellgroup.com/amyjmalay
@joinmeonthejourney

♥ ♥ ♥

#HeNeverStopsWorking

♥ ♥ ♥

Contents

Dedication ix
Special Thanks xi
Author – Amy J. Malay xiv
Author – Jebastin J. Malay xvi
1. The Day We Met 3
2. Earlier Overseas Experiences 15
3. The Hope of Beauty from Ashes 33
4. The Mission Field at Home 45
5. Letters, Letters, and More Letters 57
6. Losses & A Trip to India 79
7. Time for Transformation 93
8. Seek and You Shall Find 107
9. Some Surprises 117
10. Dream Week 131
11. Goodbye… For Now 153
12. Leftover Baskets of Provision 161
13. Staying Connected 171
14. It's the Little Things… 181
15. Learning to Turn 191
16. Meaningful Words 201
17. The Power of Testimonies 209
Our Great Cloud of Witnesses 223
Helpful Resources 257

Dedication

We dedicate this shared testimony to "Any" and "Konjjt," the two princesses we currently sponsor, and to the many thousands of other children being supported all over the world through various child sponsorship programs.

♥ ♥ ♥

x

Special Thanks

Thank you, Jesus, our Savior. This is YOUR story of love, faithfulness, and ongoing transformation in our lives. It is a gift we have been slowly unwrapping, enjoying, and sharing with others. It is a gift we will continue to unwrap for years to come.

Thank you, Patrick and Lavanya, for your support and love.

Thank you to the many friends and family members who have walked with us and are still walking with us on this journey – our cloud of witnesses.

Thank you, Sarah, for speaking out the Lord's prompting to write this story, and for taking the photo used for this book's cover.

Thank you, Julia, Kira, Nathan, and Debby, for your creative and technical editing assistance.

Thank you, Blessed Man Branding Services, for the beautiful cover design.

♥ ♥ ♥

Author Prefaces & Bios

Author — Amy J. Malay

The seed was planted in my heart years ago to write a book. I hoped and prayed that, one day, my story would blossom into one that would encourage others in their faith. Well, "one day" has arrived.

That seed was buried in the soil of my life. It was watered by many tears – my own and those of others. It was fed, and a seedling began to grow because of challenges in my life. And now, I

> *He comforts us in all our troubles so that we can comfort others. When they are troubled, we will be able to give them the same comfort God has given us.*
>
> 2 Corinthians 1:4 NLT

pray that the seedling has become a tree that bears fruit and provides shade – and perhaps even comfort – for others. The story contained in these pages is a story of God's faithfulness – in my life and in my son's life. I hope it draws your thoughts to His faithfulness in your own life as well. He *truly* never stops working.

Amy lives in Mount Joy, Pennsylvania, USA. She has served at a faith-based financial planning firm, Ambassador Advisors, since 2006. She is an Executive Director with The John Maxwell Team, and a team leader and educator with Young Living Essential Oils. Amy has a passion for speaking and training in the US and internationally. She especially enjoys sharing on topics of leadership and personal or spiritual growth.

Amy attends Mount Joy Mennonite Church. She serves preschool children in Sunday School and youth in grades 6-12 in a youth ministry. She and her husband, Patrick, will celebrate their 22nd wedding anniversary in September 2020.

♥ ♥ ♥

Author – Jebastin J. Malay

I know from experience – God is working in our lives even when we are not living for him. Nothing we can do can change His plan for our life or His love for us. Jesus has done so many good things in my life.

I wrote all about many of those good things in this book, one more of the many books that testify of all the things that Jesus has done. As you read the story, I hope you can understand His unconditional love and support

> *Jesus also did many other things. If they were all written down, I supposed the whole world could not contain the books that would be written.*
>
> John 21:25 NLT

in my life. I hope that this shared testimony will cause your mind and heart to look back to Jesus.

Jebastin lives in Chennai, Tamil Nadu, India. He served as an Accountant in a Chartered Accountant office for four years. In June 2020, he began serving as an Accountant at Christian Missions Charitable Trust, and in July 2020, he formed a small business called Tower Consulting, through which he provides accounting and business services to nonprofit organizations. He became a member of The John Maxwell Team in February 2020.

He attends Madras Pentecostal Church, where his family has attended for four generations. He serves through skit writing, prayer ministry, and videography.

He is engaged to be married to Lavanya, his sweetheart since 2014. A 2020 wedding is planned.

♥ ♥ ♥

Chapter 1

♥

The Day We Met

1. The Day We Met

It was 11:30 pm. We were a little more than half-way through a three-week visit to India, soon to arrive in the city of Chennai. I was with my mother, Jo-Ann, and an Indian friend and ministry leader, Sarah, who was accompanying us (more about her ministry to come later).

Mom, Sarah, and me just before the flight to Chennai.

As the plane landed, my heart and mind were filled with anticipation. You see, I was about to meet Jebastin, the child I had been writing to for almost 20 years. He was now a young man and had started calling me "mom" a little more than a year before. The significant moment we had both been waiting for was now only minutes away! As I waited to deplane, my mind was racing. He sent me this text just before our flight (before he knew there was a 45-minute delay):

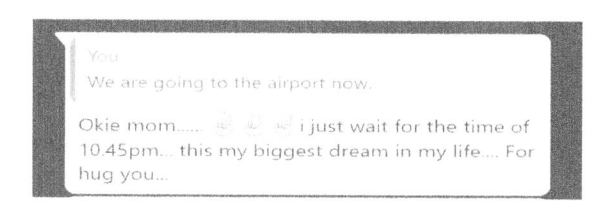

> You
> We are going to the airport now.
>
> Okie mom...... i just wait for the time of 10.45pm... this my biggest dream in my life.... For hug you...

Our flight had already been delayed by about 45 minutes. How long would it take to get our bags? I knew Jebastin would be waiting just outside the airport exit. Would I spot him first, or would he spot me first? The baggage claim area was not crowded and there were large windows. I looked out, thinking I might catch a glimpse of him. There was a small crowd, but no, I could not tell if he was there or not. The bags arrived quickly. We collected them and walked outdoors.

I continued to scan the small crowd of those waiting for family and friends. Still, I did not catch sight of Jebastin. We kept walking. And then, I caught movement out of the corner of my eye. Jebastin and his friend were rushing over to where we were. He was all smiles - and so was I! He presented me with a beautiful bouquet of sparkly orange flowers.

When he offered me a handshake along with the flowers, I pulled him in for the hug he had been dreaming about for so long. We hugged and we smiled… on our faces and in our hearts! We quickly took care of introductions for everyone else – his friend Suresh, my mom, and Sarah – and then started walking to Suresh's vehicle.

We chatted as we walked to the vehicle. The guys loaded our luggage, and then we were on our way to the hotel. Jebastin sat in the front seat to navigate the GPS while Suresh drove. The three of us ladies were in the back seat. I kept looking at him and wondering what he was thinking. Occasionally, he would look back with a grin. And I grinned back.

The car ride conversation was mostly about the traffic and the climate. At one point, Jebastin asked where the rest of our team was. We told him they had gone back to the US. I saw the surprised look on his face and my heart melted. I realized it had just dawned on him that we were there in Chennai for him. Our time there was not part of the group's mission trip, but a very intentional extension of the trip to spend time with him.

We arrived at the hotel and checked in. As I filled out my address and other personal information on the check-in form, Jebastin was standing at the counter with me. He was watching me write. I was thinking about how many times I had written to him in letters from so far away. And now I was writing while he was standing right there beside me.

After the room check-in was all set, we went up to the room. We had a short time to visit while we waited for an extra bed to be brought to the room.

First photo together!

We remembered then to take a photo – our first photo together in the same room!

I felt sad that we had such a short time to spend together that night. But it was late, and we were all tired, so we said goodnight. As we ladies settled into our room and got ready for bed, I treasured the memories of the day and anticipated more to be made in the week ahead... I also found myself pondering the history of my connection with Jebastin – all the parts of my story (and his) that led up to "the day we met."

The day I met my mom, I left home at 9 pm and arrived at the airport with my friend, Suresh, at 10:15. I looked at the flight schedule and we eagerly waited for my mom's 11:35 pm flight arrival. I remember practicing English phrases while we waited for the flight to arrive. All the sudden, I saw her coming through the airport doorway. I quickly moved to where she was walking out so I could greet her and give her flowers. It is not polite in Indian culture to hug in public, so I offered a handshake. But she hugged me instead. It was like a dream.

On the drive to the hotel, I remember asking, "Where is your team?" My mom said they had gone back to the US. And I asked, "You came here for me?" And she gave a big smile and nodded and said, "Yes, we came here to meet and visit with you!" This was when I realized she had come for me only.

When we arrived at the hotel, the others sat down to wait. I stayed with my mom at the counter while she completed the check-in. I was thanking God that she was here. She was right here in Chennai! I was watching her write in English on the check-in form, and still I felt some fear about speaking in English.

Later I was home and ready to sleep. I thought the day did not seem real! My mom was here in Chennai and she had given me the hug I had dreamed about and prayed for my entire life. I sent my mom a goodnight text… "Good night… have sweet dreams."

♥ ♥ ♥

Pause to Ponder

Think of a time when you were filled with anticipation.

What was the occasion?

How long did you wait for that day?

What surprised you?

What disappointed you?

♥ ♥ ♥

Noteworthy Notes

Chapter 2

♥

Earlier Overseas Experiences

2. Earlier Overseas Experiences

I learned later in life that my mother, Jo-Ann, always wanted to serve on an overseas mission trip. She loved that some of her kids, including me, were able to participate in overseas trips. While she lived vicariously through us and our trips, she inwardly hoped that one day she could have the experience herself.

And she was able to do just that. Her first overseas trip was with me, to India, in early 2020.

> *Every day of my life was recorded in your book. Every moment was laid out before a single day had passed.*
>
> Psalm 139:16 NLT

I, on the other hand, have been blessed to participate in multiple trips and stateside international experiences. These experiences were part of God's amazing plan. They were part of my preparation for the amazing experience of meeting and becoming a mom to Jebastin...

June-July 1990 – First International Trip

My first international travel experience was at age 18. I had just graduated from high school and was participating in the People to People Student Ambassador Program with other students in grades 10-12.

Our trip was to Russia (U.S.S.R. at that time) for three weeks. Of course, I noticed the differences in culture - the architecture, cleanliness standards, and the language.

What I remember more, are the similarities. We were young people making friends with other young people. We all had big hopes and dreams for the future. We had fun dancing and playing sports and doing service projects together. We all valued family and pets. We had curiosity and a desire to understand each other. We all had a love for our own country and honored that in each other.

1993 to 1997 – Internship & Discipleship

During my senior year of college, because of a suggestion from my mom, I sought out and later began a volunteer internship at Eastern Mennonite Missions (EMM), a local missionary agency. That internship turned into a full-time paid position after my graduation, and the international culture of faith profoundly impacted my life.

I had recommitted my life to Christ about a year before the internship began. As I worked and prayed and learned spiritual disciplines from mature believers (my colleagues at EMM), my walk with Christ grew by

> *Keep putting into practice all you have learned and received from me – everything you heard from me and saw me doing…*
>
> Philippians 4:9 NLT

leaps and bounds. During our weekly staff chapel service, I faced and overcame a fear of praying out loud in front of others. I learned more about and created spiritual growth habits in my life, such as regular prayer, journaling, fasting, and Bible-reading.

All these good habits contributed to a solid foundation of knowing God's promises so I would later be able to stand firm on them. Being part of the EMM team also provided me with opportunities to learn about other cultures. I loved meeting missionaries while they were home on leave and hearing their testimonies of how God was working all around the world.

December 1995 – Jebastin's Birthday

Before I was ever aware of Jebastin's life, God was working out a plan – a plan to give me a future and a hope!

> For I know the plans I have for you, says the Lord, plans for good and not for disaster, to give you a future and a hope.
>
> Jeremiah 29:11 NLT

Jebastin was born in Chennai, India, in December of 1995. He was the second child of his parents. His mother was a Christian. She suffered from heart issues and was frequently in and out of the hospital. Because of this, Jebastin's grandma and aunt often helped to care for him and his older sister. His younger brother was born five years later.

Also in 1995, I purchased a brown stuffed bear for the back window of my car. I named the bear Benjamin and my younger sister, Julia (age 8 at the time), called him "Benny." I chose the name Benjamin because I liked the name and thought I might use that name for a child, when and if I had a son someday.

I do not recall what happened to Benny over the years, although I do remember he got "sunburned" from being in the back window. This seemingly insignificant purchase came to my mind while writing this book. The significance will become clear to you in a later chapter.

January 1996 — Pilgrimage to The Holy Land

Just fifteen days after Jebastin's birth, I experienced another mile marker in my faith journey. I went on a ten-day pilgrimage to Israel with my friend and colleague, Mary Jane, and about thirty others.

Israel trip with Mary Jane

My appreciation for different cultures grew again as I experienced the sights, sounds, tastes, and terrain of the land where Jesus was born, and where He walked and talked. Where He slept and ate. Where He spent time with His earthly family and friends and disciples. Where He taught and healed. Where He demonstrated His great love for us by choosing to submit to death on a cross so that we could have eternal life.

> *They were now on the way up to Jerusalem, and Jesus was walking ahead of them. The disciples were filled with awe…*
>
> Mark 10:32 NLT

Like the disciples who followed Jesus "up to Jerusalem," I was filled with awe. Now, when I read my Bible, all the places we visited come alive. Places like Tel Aviv, Joppa, Caesarea, Mount Carmel, Capernaum, the Sea of Galilee, Nazareth, Jerusalem, Qumran, the Jordan River, Bethlehem, the Mount of Olives, the Mount of Beatitudes, the Dead Sea, the Garden of Gethsemane.

January 1997 to February 1998 — A "Short-Term" Trip

The following year, I learned of a short-term service trip to YWAM (Youth With a Mission) St. Croix, US Virgin Islands. More than twenty people from several local churches in my area traveled to the Caribbean for a ten-day service project trip. We painted; we removed weeds and brush with machetes; we scrubbed - indoors and out; we prepared meals; we made repairs; and all the while we were learning about the ministry of YWAM in the islands and around the world.

We also learned about the staffing needs of the training center in St. Croix. I remember one conversation with one of the staff members. He asked me, "If God asked you to jump off a cliff, would you do it?" This question truly had me thinking. Would I? Was my faith strong enough to pass such a test?

Even before returning home from the work trip to St. Croix, I felt a "nudge" to go back to serve on staff at the YWAM center, to take the leap, so to speak. As I continued to explore the opportunity, I felt God's leading as doors were opened and challenges were overcome. What started as a short-term trip had now turned into a continuing adventure.

I returned to St. Croix in April 1997. Leaving my family was difficult for me, especially when I thought about my younger siblings growing up "without" me.

Yet I knew God was calling me, and so I said "YES" to His leading. I jumped off the cliff of the unknown and landed as an accountant in the YWAM office. I also served with the children and youth at King's Kids Camp and on the worship team for the church that met at the YWAM center. I loved the time I spent there that summer and could not wait for the Discipleship Training School (DTS) to begin in September.

The DTS included three months of full-time discipleship training, followed by two months of full-time outreach. The training portion of the DTS provided another significant mile marker in my spiritual growth and healing. My identity in Christ became a firm foundation as I learned to apply more and more truths from Scripture. I dug deep into the well of

> *I will praise God's name with singing, and I will honor Him with thanksgiving. For this will please the Lord... The humble will see their God at work and be glad. Let all who seek God's help be encouraged. For the Lord hears the cries of the needy...*
>
> Psalm 69:30, 32-33 NLT

forgiveness for the wrongs done to me and for the wrongs I had done. I found freedom and joy as I worshipped and submitted my life to His rebuilding plans.

My future husband, Patrick, also attended the DTS. I did not realize it (that he was my future husband) immediately, but Pat did. He says he knew the moment he saw me. I was so focused on the Lord and the healing work He was doing in my life, that my mind was not at all on romance. In fact, I had stopped thinking about meeting the right person. At age 25, I had been frustrated up to that point with the long wait. But growing in my relationship with God had become my priority.

All the members of our team learned to know each other deeply during the DTS. We bonded over time spent together in worship, prayer, and ministry. We also shared our life stories with each other. I remember my heart breaking and at the same time rejoicing when Pat shared his testimony with the group. By God's grace, he had overcome many obstacles, and God's handiwork was evident in His life. He was truly a new

> *I will make rivers flow on barren heights, and springs within the valleys. I will turn the desert into pools of water, and the parched ground into springs… so that people may see and know, may consider and understand, that the hand of the Lord has done this, that the Holy One of Israel has created it.*
>
> Isaiah 41.18, 20 NIV

creation in Christ, an example of someone who had been transformed.

Toward the end of the training time, Pat invited me to sit down and chat. It was the first time we had a private conversation. We talked about our testimonies, our families, our dreams and hopes for the future, and more! Four hours later the "chat" ended, but something new had begun. The whole time we were talking, I was wondering what God was up to. Pat and I had many dreams in common, including a dream to serve the Lord as missionaries, and a dream to have lots of children. There were still questions in our minds, and yet God had begun to show us that He had a plan for us to serve together.

The two-month outreach portion of the DTS was an amazing multi-cultural experience. Our team travelled to two other Caribbean islands (St. Maarten and Anguilla) for about one month and then to Asia (Thailand and Vietnam) for another month. We preached and performed skits and spent time with children at various schools. We completed work projects. We taught English and shared testimonies. We went on prayer walks. We met with believers to encourage and pray for them. The trip was not without its challenges. Everyone on our team grew in spiritually through the many ministry experiences we shared.

Pat and I both particularly loved Thailand – the "Land of Smiles." While we were there, we decided we would get married later that year in September, and then return to Thailand to teach English and share God's love alongside the believers we met and had grown to love.

February 1998 to September 2001 – Engaged, Married & On a Mission!

After our DTS graduation, Pat and I were officially engaged to be married, and had a desire to return to Thailand after our wedding. During our six-month engagement, we spent time with friends and family in both Pennsylvania and South Carolina and continued to participate in activities that would prepare us for our time overseas. We participated in Alpha Ministry and took a discipleship class.

After our wedding day that September, we traveled to Thailand multiple times. In between trips to Thailand, we took a TESOL (Teaching English to Speakers of Other Languages) course through YWAM in Pennsylvania, and a discipleship course through Victory Churches International in Canada. On multiple occasions, other young adults accompanied us on the trips to

Thailand. The trips were not only a way for us to serve – but a way for us to mentor and disciple others and give them the opportunity to explore God's calling on their lives.

♥ ♥ ♥

Pause to Ponder

What experience or events in your life prepared you for something to come later?

When did you realize the connection?

How has God used that preparation to help you say "yes" to opportunities?

♥ ♥ ♥

Noteworthy Notes

Chapter 3

♥

The Hope of Beauty from Ashes

3. The Hope of Beauty from Ashes

I remember walking with my mom as a very young child from our home to my grandma's home for visits. My mom believed in Jesus, and so I also believed in Jesus ever since I can remember.

Jebastin's Indian parents

When she would kneel to pray, I remember sitting up on her shoulders.

I remember times when my dad would hit my mom. When that happened, we would go to my grandma's house. My older sister stayed at my grandma's house almost all the time, and when my younger brother was born, he stayed there too.

But I stayed at home with my mom and dad. I always felt like I was not loved by my grandma as much as my sister and brother were loved.

2001 to 2002 – Where Is My Mom?

My mom got sick when I was five years old, and I remember her being in a wheelchair. Something was wrong with her

> I will not abandon you as orphan – I will come to you.
>
> John 14:18 NLT

heart and she did not get proper treatment. My younger brother was just a baby then – less than a year old when our mom died at age 33. I remember seeing her in a freezer box (like a coffin) after she died, but I thought she was asleep. I talked to her, and family and friends came to pay their respects to her while she was in the freezer box in front of the home. I also remember going to the burial service, but I still did not understand that my mother had died.

For about six months after she died, I stayed with my father at our home. I remember walking to school alone and seeing the other kids with their mothers. At lunch time, other kids' mothers would come for lunch, and I ate alone. I wondered why my mom did not come. Where was she? I felt very lonely.

One night, I woke up and went searching for my mother. I left the house to look for her. I did not find her and could not find my way home in the dark. I asked a man sleeping on the street for help. He walked with me to help me find my way back home.

The next morning, my father took me to my grandma's house. I stayed at her home all the time after that.

September 11, 2001 – 9/11

In 2001, we were using our home in the United States as a missions training center. We had hoped it would serve as a home base for taking teams on short-term trips to Thailand. On the night of September 11, 2001, we lost that home and most of our possessions to an electrical fire. This happened in the late evening on the same day as the 9/11 terrorist attack on the United States.

Fire damage to our home, September 11, 2001

No one was injured in the fire, and for that we were grateful. I am also grateful that many of our photos were saved – thanks mom! However, the fire, along with the heaviness our country was experiencing due to 9/11, began a season of struggle in our lives.

Poor choices my husband made at that time impacted me also. The specifics of those choices and their consequences are another story altogether – perhaps even another book!

For my part, it was like my dreams were dying a slow death. The loss of our home and possessions was one thing, but the real heartache for me was the loss of what I thought our marriage and life together would be – a partnership in ministry.

Over the next number of years, while my husband dealt with some of his own battles, I grieved the loss of that dream of serving overseas full-time. I was in survival mode, clinging to my faith with all the strength I could find, and praying that He would help me to understand His plan. I hoped that one day He would bring beauty from the ashes of my life.

> *But those who trust in the Lord will find new strength. They will soar high on wings like eagles. They will run and not grow weary. They will walk and not faint.*
>
> Isaiah 40.31 NLT

I participated in Bible studies at various churches and through a ministry called "Celebrate Recovery." I leaned hard on the spiritual disciplines that had been modeled for me by others in my family and by those I had met in my earlier "preparation" experiences. I stood firm on the promises of God's Word, and HE was truly my strength.

♥ ♥ ♥

Pause to Ponder

What loss in your life have you grieved?

How have you seen God working during a painful experience?

What are some of the habits that helped you cope during a painful time in life?

♥ ♥ ♥

Noteworthy Notes

Chapter 4

♥

The Mission Field at Home

4. The Mission Field at Home

As time went by, I remember crying out to God to ask Him to give me wisdom so that I would know what I should do – now that I was "alone" in the desire to continue with missionary work. My heart had always been to share His love with others, and now it seemed evident that I would not be traveling overseas anymore.

I remember God speaking to my heart that my mission field was now at home. It struck me that I did not need to go *overseas* to find ministry opportunities. The struggles Pat faced in his own life were ongoing and brought opportunities knocking – right on the front door of my heart. I had asked God to use me as a vessel of His love. Was I willing to love intentionally and unconditionally in my own home, in my own family, in my own neighborhood?

And, as I said yes to His call before, I again said, "Yes. Here I am Lord. Send me. Use me. Help me to love unconditionally. Help me to be that vessel of Your love, by Your strength."

> Then I heard the Lord asking, "Whom should I send as a messenger to this people? Who will go for us?" I said, "Here I am. Send me."
>
> Isaiah 6:8 NLT

As always, He was working. I know he heard my prayers, and by His grace, I found many opportunities to serve well on the mission field at home.

2003 – An At-Home Opportunity

I learned about Compassion International in early 2003 and requested information about sponsoring a child. I saw this as an opportunity to be a vessel of His love to a child in need. I did not choose a child to sponsor like you sometimes can at events where an array of photos is on display. I did not ask for a child with a certain birthday. I did not ask for a boy or a girl. I did not ask for a child from any certain country. Instead, when I filled out the reply form and mailed it to Compassion, I checked the box that said, "I'd like to sponsor a child that has been waiting for a sponsor." I trusted that the Lord would assign to me the child He wanted me to have. And that is just what happened.

Pat and Amy, 2003

I received a photo of Jebastin, along with a welcome letter in mid-March 2003. He would have been 7 years old at that time. The letter read, in part: *Your sponsorship will bring great joy to Jebastin and will impact his life forever. We have reserved the sponsorship of Jebastin just for you. It is our hope that you will be the one who will identify with this child, love him, pray for him, and provide the support needed so he can participate in the program.*

I wrote the first letter to Jebastin soon after that to introduce myself and Pat and to let him know we were praying for him. Pat was supportive of the sponsorship, but still primarily dealing with his own struggles during this time. I was the one that wrote the letters, and I signed them from "Aunty Amy and Uncle Pat."

I do not have a copy of the first letter, and, of course, I did not know a lot about Jebastin at that point. I knew that he lived with his grandparents and that his life could not be easy. Otherwise, he would not be in the program. In that first letter, I included Jeremiah 29:11.

This promise from God's Word had been (and still is!) an ongoing source of hope in my own heart. I wanted to inspire hope in Jebastin's young heart, too. That welcome letter from Compassion, along with the photo they sent me was the start of the "file" in my home office for Jebastin, #IN-518-0018.

> *For I know the plans I have for you, says the Lord, plans for good and not for disaster, to give you a future and a hope.*
>
> Jeremiah 29:11 NLT

And with that first verse sent from my heart to his, a seed of HOPE was planted in both our hearts. You see, as always, God was working. I would not find out how until many years later.

2003 – I Got A Mom!

After my birth mother died, a teacher in the Compassion center, who had been a friend of my mother's, helped my aunt with placing me in Compassion. I remember going to the center with my aunt. There were many other children there. We were all in line to get our pictures taken. After they took my picture, we left.

A few days later, they contacted me and said I was accepted into the program and that a sponsor would be found for me. Now, I could go to the center every day after school. Only one child per family could be placed with the Compassion program. By God's grace, he chose me.

The first time I went there, I played with other kids. There was a meeting for the children. The group was split up by class (grade). I was in Class 1, about age 5. There were two hundred seventy-nine children in my center, and there were two hundred sixty-two sponsors.

After some months went by, I remember getting my first sponsor letter from Amy Malay. I remember thinking "I got a mom!" I read her letter eagerly and took note of the Bible verses she sent in the letter. I wrote back to her with help from the center teachers.

The Church where the Compassion
program was held in Chennai

♥ ♥ ♥

Pause to Ponder

Who is someone you admire for the way they are intentional to minister to those at home?

What is one at-home ministry opportunity you have in your life?

Name a few seeds of hope you have sewn into others' lives.

Noteworthy Notes

Chapter 5

♥

Letters, Letters, and More Letters

5. Letters, Letters, and More Letters

After that first letter in 2003, I wrote to Jebastin a few times each year. The first two letters I received from him were written by a social worker. The social worker commented in her second letter, "Jebastin is a promising young man with brilliance in academics." She also said, "He made a note of your names and said he would pray for you." After that, all the letters were written by him in English. His handwriting was neat, and I loved reading the letters and sometimes "decoding" what a word or phrase meant.

He always mentioned how the Bible verses I sent him were an encouragement. And I was always touched and humbled by his devoted prayers for me and my family. He loved to add drawings to his letters, and always asked for photos of me and Pat, of our pets, and of our other family members.

Jebastin's letters were always an encouragement to me. I remember being impressed with his spiritual maturity. His love for the Lord would always shine through his letters. And he always said how much he loved us and was praying for us.

Wasn't there more I could do to help him? I wondered about his day-to-day life and kept praying that the spiritual seeds planted would grow and be nurtured even though I could not be physically present in his life to see him growing in the day-to-day.

I also felt sadness when Jebastin would ask me when I was going to visit India, or when he said his grandma asked when I would be visiting. I was still in survival mode myself – emotionally and financially. This was part of the reason my letters were not as frequent as I wish they had been. Traveling overseas to meet Jebastin was something that I put out of my mind since it seemed so impossible at the time.

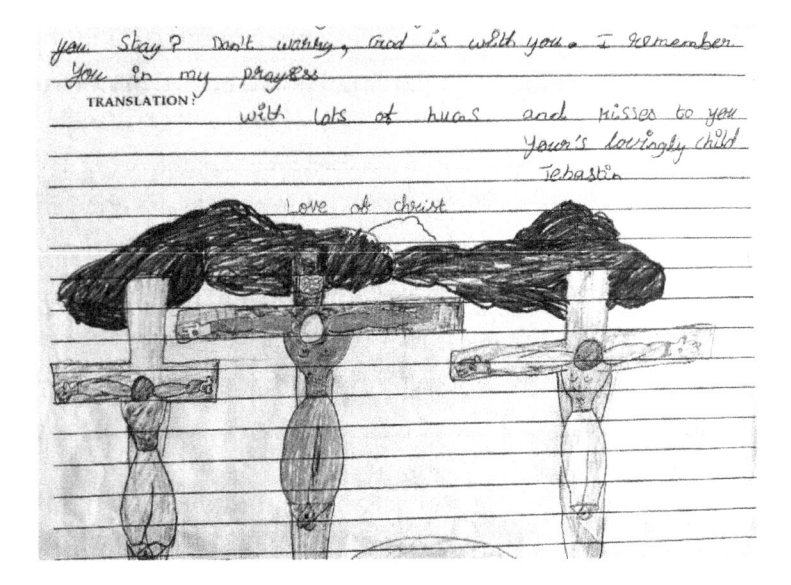

2005 – A Season of Loss

In February 2005, I was nine years old. That was the time my grandfather died. Our family situation changed personally and financially. I loved my grandpa but had not talked or spent a lot of time with him. To me, it seemed he had more affection for my siblings, Angel and Abishek.

Every morning at 5 am we would wake up and go with my grandpa to buy milk. I remember him telling lots of stories about his life. He worked for the Electricity Board. After he retired, he felt sick. He was admitted to hospital for treatment but there was no option to help him.

When my grandpa died, I did not cry. I do not know why, but I have never cried for any death in my home. My family grieved for my grandpa for a year, but I quickly moved on from the sorrows. Perhaps my mother's death made my heart like stone. I always thought we just needed to move on with reality. I thought all the sadness was a waste of time, so I did not allow myself to feel grief.

2005 to 2008 – Where is My Dad?

My birth father came twice a month to visit me until I was about ten years old. After that, he visited only every six months or so until I was about 13. Then, he rarely came to visit. He was struggling. He had chosen a life of drinking alcohol and could not care for me.

> Lord, you know the hopes of the helpless. Surely you will hear their cries and comfort them. You will bring justice to the orphans...
>
> Psalm 10:17-18 NLT

My life was very hard during this time. I was told to study hard because I did not have a mother or a good father. Even though my mom's relatives took us in, I did not feel loved. I always felt that preference was given to their own children. I was yelled at harshly even for what I felt were small mistakes.

THE **HUNGER** FOR **LOVE** IS MUCH MORE DIFFICULT TO REMOVE THAN THE HUNGER FOR BREAD.

Lee Teresa

2006 – Christian Camp & A Commitment to Christ

When I was nine, I went to a summer Bible camp through my church and learned about missionary stories. I wanted to be like a missionary, and I asked Jesus into my heart at that camp. I told God I wanted to be a missionary. Isaiah 41:10 is a promise verse I received at that time.

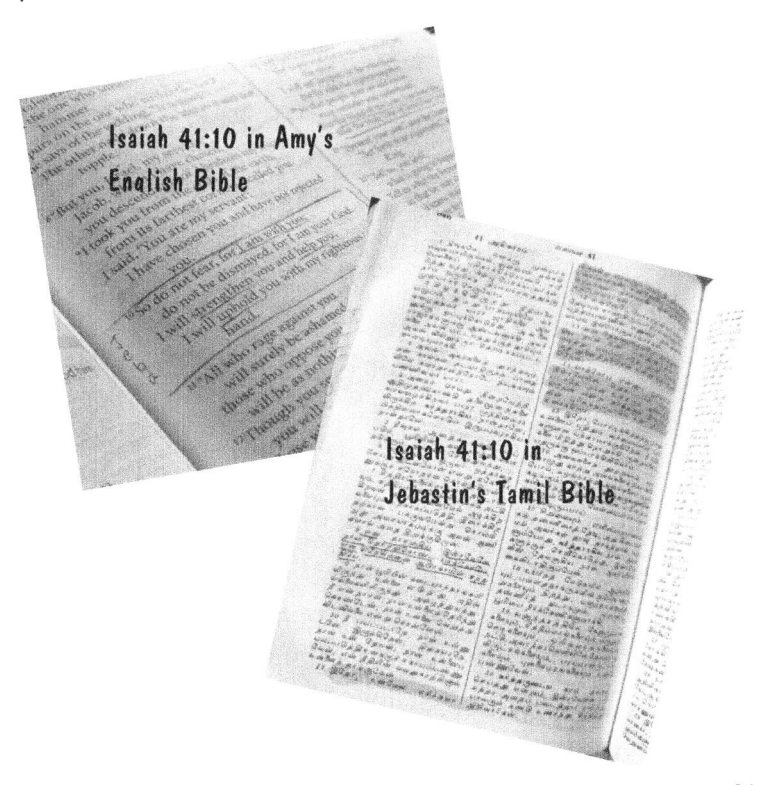

> *Don't be afraid, for I am with you. Don't be discouraged, for I am your God. I will strengthen you and help you. I will hold you up with my victorious right hand.*
>
> Isaiah 41.10 NLT

Isaiah 41:10 in Amy's English Bible

Isaiah 41:10 in Jebastin's Tamil Bible

2007 – Have You Got a Child or Not?

Jebastin asked in one letter, "Please tell me have you got a child or not?" Having children had been my heart's desire for a long time, so his question struck a pain point in my own heart. I had always pictured myself getting married, having kids, and raising them to follow God.

In my mind, my full-time work outside of the home was temporary. It was something I would do only until we had children to raise. I viewed raising children as the true and most meaningful work of life. When I wrote Jebastin back and answered his question, he wrote back in his next letter that he would be praying for us to have children.

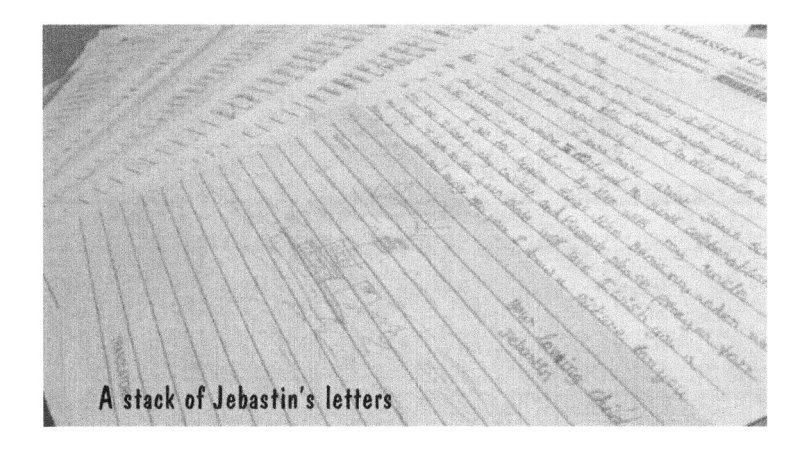

A stack of Jebastin's letters

Years continued to pass by, and my life was routine. I continued serving God in a series of full-time jobs during the day. On weekends and during the evenings, I took walks, spent time with family, and found other ways to serve. I served at church by teaching kids in Sunday School, Vacation Bible School, and other activities. I had several part-time business pursuits. These businesses were like my "babies." The time I spent on business was sort of like a "replacement" for the time I might have spent with children if we had them.

All the while, I continued to wonder why God said "no" to my desire for children. All the while, I continued to write letters and pray for Jebastin. And all the while, God was working.

2007 to 2008 – School & Compassion Center Routine

I used to write five or six pages for the draft of my letters to my mom. The teachers told me to skip some of what I wrote for the final letter to be sent. It ended up being one or two pages. I wanted to write more than one or two pages, but there was a limit of space for the letters. I was waiting every day for photos and letters from my mom. I went to the center every day after school and each day I would wonder if there would be a letter for me.

Jebastin, 2007

I enjoyed the activities and was provided with an evening meal each day at the center. The teaching at the center helped me learn more about God and the truths of the Bible. I had many good friends at the Compassion center, and I am still friends with some of them today.

There were times that other Compassion sponsors would come to visit the center. The sponsored child would spend a whole day with their sponsor. This is one of the reasons

I always asked in my letters when my mom was going to visit India. I prayed for my mom every night before bed. I never knew what to pray for specifically, so I just prayed that God would help her. And I prayed that she would visit India someday.

During my school years, my schedule was very routine. I would normally wake up at 6 am for Bible reading and prayer. Then I would get ready for school. After school, I walked four or five kilometers with my friend to visit his home. When we got to his home, we went to the Compassion center to play cricket. After that, the teaching program would start, and usually we had a meal. Then we would hang around for an hour or so with my friends. After that, I would go home for the night. I spent time reading my Bible and praying before going to bed. This was my daily routine.

In the summertime, three Compassion centers combined to provide Bible quiz programs and sports tournaments for all the students. We also had Vacation Bible School in the summers. Every six months, we all went on special trips to places like theme parks, museums, a solar system theatre, a botanical garden, or the children's park. Every year we also had a spiritual retreat for three or four days. It was always in a different location. Through all these experiences, I learned many things about God and the Bible. I enjoyed every moment I spent at the Compassion center.

2007 to 2008 – I am Fine by the Grace of God

While we wrote letters back and forth, Jebastin called me Aunty and so "nephew" is how I thought of him. We had a very warm and prayerful writing relationship. No letter went out without a mention of praying for the other person. In many of his letters, Jebastin used the phrase, "I am fine by the Grace of God."

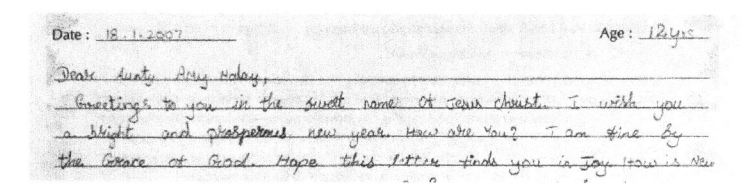

> Date: 18.1.2007   Age: 12 yrs
> Dear Aunty Pray Holay,
> Greetings to you in the sweet name of Jesus christ. I wish you a bright and prosperous new year. How are you? I am fine by the Grace of God. Hope this letter finds you in Joy. How is New

I loved that he said it this way. It was an indicator to me of how much he relied on God despite difficulties in his life. I did not share much of my testimony with him. I did not want to burden this child already in a life of struggle with struggles I was facing in my own life.

His repeated statement, "I am fine by the Grace of God" resonated with me. I knew the same was true in my life. In fact, my middle name, Janelle, means "God is gracious" or "God is merciful." I know with certainty that God's grace is what carried me through the difficult seasons of my life. In fact, many people, upon hearing a part of my testimony would ask me, "How do you do it?" or "How can you do this?" The only response I could ever think of was "by God's grace."

Without His promises and His faithfulness to keep them; without Him holding me up; without His constant encouragement and strength; without His reassurance and love; without His amazing peace that surpasses all understanding; without any of these I could not survive. But with GOD, I can not only survive, but THRIVE! And I knew the same faithful God was carrying Jebastin through the struggles in his life.

Some things about my life I shared only with my sponsor; no one else. Ever since the beginning, I thought of Amy as my mom. But in the letters, I called her aunty since that was the cultural way to address someone in India. I was so happy when I received her letters and thought to myself, "My mom is writing to me."

When I was nine years old, I wrote in one of my letters (pictured above), "Sometimes I feel like an orphan. But it is very encouraging for me to think that you are there to love me! Thank you for your love and care." Later, when I was 11, I wrote, "Please tell me have you got a child or not?" When she sent her next letter and said that she did not have children, I remember writing back to her and saying, "I am your child, don't worry."

When I was about 14, I wrote a thank you note (pictured below) for a birthday gift I had received. I said, "Many are the times I become sad because I am motherless. My father also does not take care of me. But I thank God that He has given me a loving sponsor (you)."

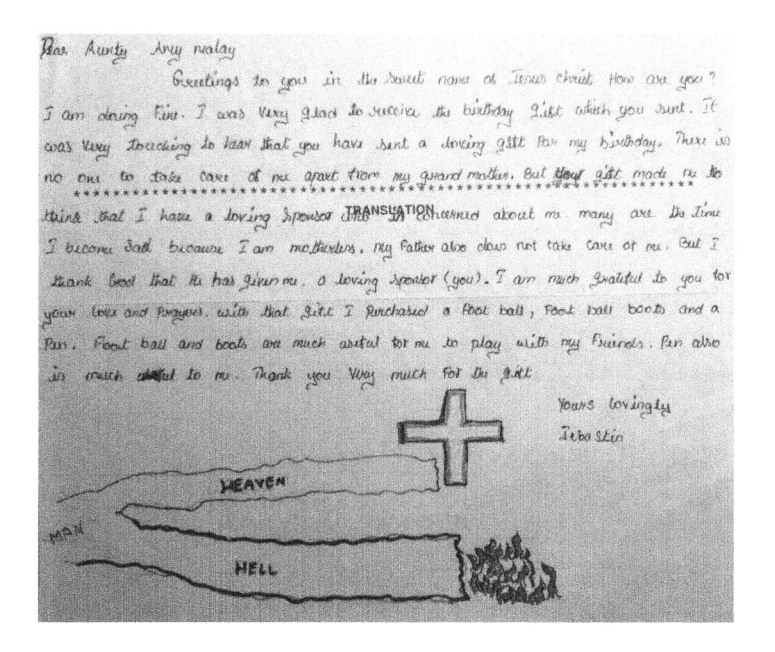

I dreamed of the day when I would meet my sponsor — my mom. I prayed about this every day.

2009 to 2014 — A House Guest

My husband's father, Don, lived at our home for five years. This was at a time when he could no longer live alone due to dementia and declining physical strength. It was challenging, yet a wonderful time of reconnection between my husband and his father. And a chance for me to truly get to know the father-in-law I had only met briefly before that. His presence brought an additional level of joy to our home.

Patrick and his father, Don, on Don's 86th birthday, 2011

Two of the letters from Jebastin in 2010 were signed, "With Love Your Son, Jebastin" and "Your Loving Son, Jebastin." He was 15 years old. I do not recall this phrasing impacting me at the time. When I looked back later at the letters (in preparation for this book), and read them in succession, I was amazed at some of the details I did not remember.

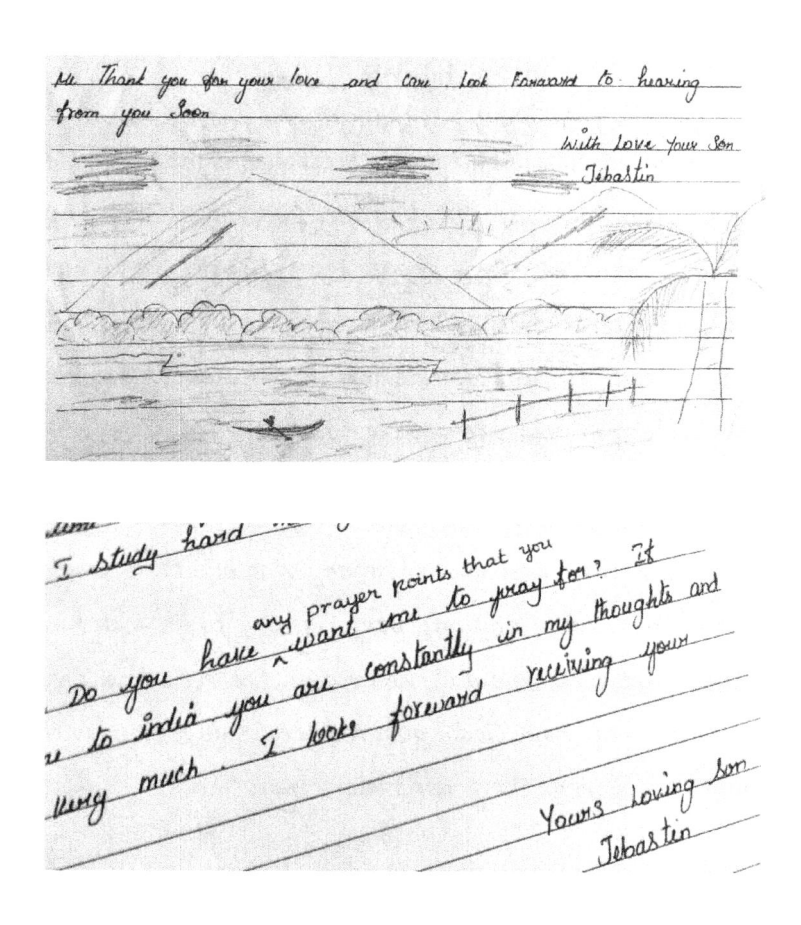

In 2012, I also received a letter from the Compassion center facilitator. Part of the letter read, "It is through your support and encouragement that Jebastin is able to progress and look at life in a different way. Sponsors like you have transformed the lives of children and their families." The words in this letter, along with Jebastin's own letters, encouraged me and helped me to know that my seemingly small efforts (letters and monthly financial support) were, in fact, making a difference.

Do you remember Benny the bear?

2012 – Jebastin "Benny"

I had wanted to get baptized since I was eight years old. Every time someone got baptized in my church, my pastor shared the story about Jesus' baptism and how God said from heaven, "This is my son, in whom I am well pleased." I kept wondering if that would happen when it was my turn to get baptized.

One time I heard a story about a poor orphan boy in Scotland named Benjamin. The boy was blind. He would go to church every day and pray for God to be with him and protect him. One day, he crossed the road and died in an accident. And God appeared, and said, "I am with you. Don't worry. There is no more pain."

When I heard this story, I decided that when I was old enough to get baptized, I would take the Christian name Benjamin. In India, many people take a Christian name when they get baptized because their given name might be a Hindu name. When I got baptized, I did take this name. Many people still do not call me this name, but I love it. After my baptism, I felt very close to God, like I had a new life in my relationship with Him.

♥ ♥ ♥

Pause to Ponder

Which Bible verse would you consider to be a "promise verse" in your life?

What have you prayed for years and perhaps it seems like there is no answer?

What does baptism represent to you?

♥ ♥ ♥

Noteworthy Notes

Chapter 6

♥

Losses & A Trip to India

6. Losses & A Trip to India

2014 – News from Compassion and a Series of Deaths

In 2014, I started receiving emails from Compassion indicating that they were praying about the situation in India, and they hoped to be able to keep their centers open. I did not understand what the situation was but prayed along with them for the program to continue. Jebastin was 19 years old, and I also thought he might age out of the program soon. I was not sure what would happen.

At the end of 2014, Pat's father, Don, died in our home. He had been declining in strength and bedridden for months. In September, he began receiving hospice care, and died in early November.

We had two small dogs – Sugar and Pepper - that were very close to Don. They were best buddies and spent all day every day with him. A short time after Don's passing, Sugar died in Pat's arms while I was at work. On top of the recent loss of Don, it was devastating. And then within another few months Pepper died. This series of deaths was like one punch after another. It was very hard, and Pat began to suffer from debilitating depression. It was hard for me, too, and I again felt like we were in survival mode. But I had learned how to "carry on" during difficult circumstances, and that is what I did.

2015 – A Trip to India

A short time later, in early 2015, my sister Julia participated in a trip to India. I wanted to go, too, but it was not realistic given the recent losses that we had just experienced.

I remember following Julia's posts during her trip. I prayed for her and the others on the trip. I thought of Jebastin and wondered whether their visit was close to his location.

During the first few days of her trip to India, Julia met Sarah Rhakho (the same Sarah from the very first chapter of this book), a ministry leader serving poor students and families in the city of Delhi. Sarah had recently opened St. Matthew School, a Christian nonprofit. At the school, the Bible is taught to the students and shared with many of the students' families, too. Hospital visitations, patient advocacy, family visitations, and prayer are all part of this ministry. Sarah also directs Vacation Bible School in the slum areas.

Julia was deeply moved by Sarah's heart and ministry and after returning from her trip, she wrote about Sarah:

> *Sarah is IN THE TRENCHES. She is DOING THE WORK. She is sustained by the energy and grace of Jesus as she works day to day to further His kingdom. This woman has done much, with little. When I stood in the street with her saying goodbye, she looked at me earnestly and asked, "When will you come back?" I hugged her tightly as the cars zoomed past and caught our scarves in the polluted breeze. "I do not know, Sarah, but I promise I will find a way to send you some help. I promise you. I will not forget you!"*

And so, Julia came back from that trip with a passion to support Sarah's ministry in any way that she could. One of the ways she began supporting Sarah was through the proceeds from her independent business with Young Living Essential Oils. Because of Julia's essential oils education efforts, I later became part of Julia's team with Young Living, which meant that I, too, was supporting Sarah's ministry in Delhi.

As always, God was working. Julia's trip to India during this season, and the connections she made there, were seeds planted for a future connection that we knew nothing about... yet.

You might be wondering, what are essential oils? The short version is: Essential oils are the life blood – the most powerful part – of plants. They are mentioned in the Bible more than 1,100 times. They are God's provision for the natural support of our bodily systems.

If you are curious, a link for more information is included in the "Helpful Resources" section at the end of this book. You can also learn more by finding and following Julia's essential oils education account on Instagram: @oilygoodlife.

2014 to 2015 — Devastating Losses

Around 2014 or 2015, the Compassion center stopped providing meals for the students in the evenings. Only snacks were provided for the last 2-3 years that the center was open.

During 2015 there was a major flood in my town. My home was covered fully with water. All of us had to stay up on the roof of the home. We made a tent for some shelter and took some of our possessions up on the roof. After that we went to stay at another relative's house until all the water was gone. This was a very difficult situation. The Compassion center provided some provisions for each student's family during this difficult time.

Around May of 2016, I was contacted and told to come and complete my letters so that they could be sent to my sponsor. Two hundred eighty-five students were there at the time the center was closed. All of us were left without further contact with our sponsors. A church was also operating out of the same building as the center, and now the building was being used as a church only.

The letters and photos from our sponsors were not given to the students. Everything that had arrived over the years were kept on file by the center. I froze the image of my favorite photo of my mom in my mind. I memorized my file number, IN-5180018, and I still wonder if the letters my mom wrote to me are in that file. I still hope someday I will be able to have the file. I can still picture the box that my file was in. It was on the top shelf because the files were alphabetical, so my file was near the beginning.

At the time the center closed, the loss of contact with my mom was devastating for me. She had not died, but she was "gone" just the same. I could not write letters anymore. I would not get any more letters from her. I suffered a lot and even cried because of this loss.

2016 to 2017 – A Dark Period

Sometime after that, I experienced a dark time. Depression, loneliness, and jealousy were in my life and I turned away from God. I started drinking alcohol and using some other drugs. I stopped going to church. I spent most of my time with friends who were not a good influence on me.

I am not proud of many things I did during this time. I had a lot of anger and was not kind to people that I loved. Sometimes I did not go home for a few days at a time, and I ate food out of the garbage. Occasionally, I would ask myself, "Why am I here? I don't want to live like my dad." For a long time, I ignored these questions in my mind and kept living this way.

My cousin Jerald was faithful to invite me every weekend to come back to church. He came to my home on the way to church and asked if I would come along. My heart was hard, and I said "no" every week for a long time.

♥ ♥ ♥

Pause to Ponder

Who do you know that is "in the trenches" of serving others?

How have you seen God working to provide for that person's needs? How have you seen God providing for YOUR needs?

What has caused you, or someone you know, to turn away from God?

♥ ♥ ♥

Noteworthy Notes

Chapter 7

♥

Time for Transformation

7. Time for Transformation

2016 – The Amazing JMT

I became a member of the John Maxwell Team (JMT) in early 2016, after a renewed desire for spiritual and personal growth (transformation!) was awakened in my heart. I became very intentional about this growth and devoted myself fully to taking the courses offered through the JMT program. When I attended the three-day certification event in August of that year, I felt like I had found "my kind of people." The culture of the JMT was so aligned with who I was and who I wanted to become. It was a nurturing and safe environment for me to begin to set goals again.

And now my goals included professional speaking and training. I began to volunteer for speaking opportunities in my local community. I knocked on many doors, trying to find the way He would use me best – the way He would help me leave a legacy of faith and hope.

Patrick & Amy, 2016

Early 2017 — No More Letters

After many emails and updates and prayers hoping the Compassion center would not need to close, I received a notification that the Compassion center had in fact closed. There was no access to any child's information. I was left with no expectation that I would ever meet Jebastin in person or even hear from him again. I continued to pray for him and did not really understand why the center had closed. I never searched for him. I did not believe it would be possible to find one young man in a country with more than a billion people when I knew his first name only.

This was just a few months after I laid down my desire for my own birth or adoptive children. I knew that nothing was impossible for God, and it was still a desire in my heart. However, with every year that passed it seemed more and more unlikely. Pat and I had looked into adoption possibilities a few times, especially since my family has quite a bit of familiarity with adoption and foster parenting. But those doors did not open either. And now the connection with Jebastin, the child I had sponsored for so many years, had also come to an end.

The personal growth I had been exploring and experiencing helped me with "letting go" once more. I was determined to put my trust in His plan for my life. It seemed clear that His plan was not for me to have birth children and raise them up to be followers of Christ. It also seemed clear that adoption was not His plan. So then what was the plan?

I decided to set aside the solutions I could see, and I began to seek His wisdom as to how I could leave a legacy when it seemed that my "family tree" would end with me. It was a rather painful decision-point in my life. I felt like I was giving up on my dream of being a mom. I was putting the dream on the "altar" so to speak.

I wanted my life to be used for His purposes. I wanted to pass on a legacy of standing firm on His promises. I did not know how God was going to accomplish that. It seemed impossible, but I knew His love would never fail me.

> *Jesus looked at them intently and said, "Humanly speaking, it is impossible. But with God, everything is possible."*
>
> Matthew 19:26 NLT

I decided it was time to stop "waiting for something to happen." I began knocking on doors and saying "yes" to any opportunities where the doors opened before me. I devoted myself to intentional personal and spiritual growth through the training and courses offered by the JMT. I continued volunteering as a speaker. I found ways to contribute to the development of my colleagues in the businesses with which I was involved. I prayed for wisdom and knowledge about His plan for my "legacy." The eyes of my heart were open and watching for whatever He was going to do.

2017 to 2018 — A Transformed Heart

In December of 2017, after Jerald kept inviting me, I finally agreed to go back to church with him. I had just turned 22 years old. As soon as I walked in the door, God touched my heart. He spoke the verses from Revelation 2:4-5 to my heart. I rededicated my life to Christ and took holy communion that day.

> But I have this complaint against you. You do not love me or each other as you did at first! Look how you have fallen! Turn back to me and do the works you did at first. If you do not repent, I will come and remove your lampstand from its place among the churches.
>
> Revelation 2:4-5 NLT

My old friends were still distractions in my life. Gradually, I spent more time with God and in prayer, and more time with my friends and family at church.

Jebastin & Jerald, Dec 2017

Eventually I left the old friends for good. I found out later one of them overdosed and died. All the others got into trouble with the police. I know God was protecting me. I am grateful that He got me out of that place in my life.

Now I look to God so that I can keep growing. I still sometimes have anger and He is teaching me better ways to deal with that. I pray, sing worship songs, and read the Bible as well as other books to help me learn and grow as a believer in Christ.

God also helped me to grow in my work. I was working for an auditor. He is also a Christian and many of our clients are Christian ministries. I liked this job and learned many professional skills from my boss. He was a spiritual mentor for me.

I became more involved with the youth at my church, and they are a blessing to me.

Jebastin with some of the youth, 2020

March 2018 – Transformation Costa Rica

When I heard about the transformational leadership trips that JMT members could participate in, I knew in my heart I was supposed to go on the next trip. There was no specific date yet for the next trip, but I stayed tuned in to announcements.

> Then I heard the Lord asking, "Whom should I send as a messenger to this people? Who will go for us?" I said, "Here I am. Send me."
>
> Isaiah 6:8 NLT

During 2017, the Transformation Costa Rica trip was announced for early 2018. My response was still, "Here am I, Lord, send me!"

I did not have the funding yet, but I knew that where God calls, He also provides. And He was indeed faithful to provide the funds needed. In fact, registration fees for a workshop I was presenting covered my trip expenses. The day of the workshop was the very day that registration for the Costa Rica trip opened. The trip registration date was not known ahead of time, so it was a clear sign to me that this was His provision.

I was able to join with 250 other leadership coaches in facilitating values-based roundtable discussions. It was a "train the trainer" mission. Our team trained over 14,000 leaders in less than one week!

Some of the coaches, including me, stayed an extra day after the leadership training portion of the trip. We spent the extra day teaching children and completing a painting project at a local primary school.

The Costa Rica trip was my first overseas trip since 2001. It was a "re-awakening" of my dreams for international travel and ministry. I still did not know how or where I would be going next, but I knew that, as always, God was working.

♥ ♥ ♥

Pause to Ponder

In what ways has transformation happened in your life?

In other words, which behaviors or attitudes are not the same now as they used to be?

Describe a time when you "knew in your heart" you were called to something or somewhere.

♥ ♥ ♥

Noteworthy Notes

Chapter 8

♥

Seek & You Shall Find

8. Seek and You Shall Find

By May 2018, the Compassion center had been closed for about two years. God touched my life a year or so before, and I was living for Him. I again started to wonder about my sponsor – my mom. Where is she, and what is she doing now? I got the idea to search for her name one evening. I typed her name in the search bar on Facebook. I saw the picture of the fourth person down and knew it was her. I did not send a friend request, but instead I sent a message though the Messenger app. I had installed the app on my phone only for the purpose of sending her a message. I was ecstatic to have found her and wondered if she would remember me.

> And so I tell you, keep on asking, and you will receive what you ask for. Keep on seeking, and you will find. Keep on knocking, and the door will be opened to you.
>
> Luke 11:9 NLT

Later that day, after what seemed like a very long time, she replied to my message. I jumped up and down and danced and shouted in the roads. I even kissed my friend Karthick! I was flying high like Ironman!! I did not think about her coming to India; I was just happy to find her and to be connected.

May 2018 – Did You Remember Me?

One morning in May of 2018, as I was getting ready to leave for work, I noticed a new message request in my Messenger account (the kind that is from someone that is not your "friend" on Facebook). When I looked at the message and saw who it was from, I gasped, and my hand flew up to cover my heart!

> Hai Amy anuty.... Did you remember me... Jebastin from India
>
> I happy to see in Facebook ur my sponsors
>
> How is uncle pat
>
> How sugar moose papper
>
> I daliy remember you in my prayer... Please pray for me

I was on my way out the door and running behind schedule, and I could not reply immediately. But my heart and mind were racing! Of course I remembered him! How did he find me? How had he been all this time? Later, during a break, I replied to the message.

The communication with the "refrigerator kid" I had sponsored for many years picked up with texting instead of letter writing. We now had "direct" communication with each other in real time. At first, our conversations were casual and not that frequent. We discussed the weather, time difference, and family updates.

September 2018 – Shall I Call You Mom?

Later in the year, I received a special text from Jebastin. I had just sent him a few of his childhood photos the night before. His reply the next morning was, "Good morning mom." This was the first time he called me mom. This was the first time *anyone* had authentically called me mom. I never thought anyone would *ever* call me mom. I had set aside the desire for motherhood because I thought the Lord's answer was "no."

And with that simple greeting, a surge of emotion welled up in me. The door of hope that I had closed was flung WIDE open in the split second it took me to read that greeting. The conversation went on about other topics.

Then later in the conversation, he typed, "Aunt… Shall I call you mom… Because I don't like to call you aunt." He could not see the tears in my eyes as I sent the reply, "Yes you can call me mom if you like!"

That same day, I received this photo of Jebastin with Joshua, his newest nephew, and was also assigned "grandma" status for Joshua and his older brother Caleb.

I still did not truly understand just how much he thought of me as his mom. From that point on, he still went back and forth between calling me mom and aunty. I also did not truly embrace being his mom immediately. I did not understand this as true motherhood, and I was cautious about investing my whole heart into something that I did not understand.

♥ ♥ ♥

Pause to Ponder

When was a time that someone from your past unexpectedly came back into your life?

Describe a time when something or someone caused you to gasp in surprise.

Who or what has reawakened hope in your heart?

♥ ♥ ♥

Noteworthy Notes

Chapter 9

♥

Some Surprises

9. Some Surprises

November 2018 – A Surprise Visitor

A few months after Jebastin and I were back in touch, a friend and colleague of mine, Vinodh, mentioned that he was going home to India to visit family. Vinodh and I both serve on the Culture Committee with The John Maxwell Team. As part of this committee, our goal is to promote our team's ten core values and recognize members of the team who display them.

Vinodh was not planning to be in Chennai, Jebastin's home city, on his trip, but he did have family there. Since he is the leader of our culture team, and a true carrier of our core values, I was not surprised when Vinodh graciously said he would visit Jebastin if possible. He said he considered it a blessing to be a point of connection between us, especially as someone who was familiar with the culture and could speak Jebastin's language.

I did not tell Jebastin about this possible visit since I was not sure if it would work out. Later that month, Vinodh did in fact visit Chennai. I received a text from Jebastin with a photo of them together. He was so surprised and excited to have this visit from someone that had a connection to me, and I was delighted to see the smiles on both their faces.

I never knew that my mom had friends from India. One day, a friend of hers, Vinodh, called me and introduced himself. He asked if he could meet with me. I agreed, and we decided to meet in a coffee shop called "Coffee Day."

We met there, and he gave me a gift of chocolates and candies. We had some good conversation in that coffee shop. I asked him if he could help me with something for my mom. I wanted to buy a sari for her, and he agreed to take it back to the US with him and send it to my mom.

The next morning, around 10 am, me and my cousin Jerald met with him. It was raining very heavily that morning, but we covered the package well and took it to him. He welcomed us into his uncle's home and introduced us to his family.

We talked a lot about my mom. I remember wondering before that whether my mom remembers me. When her friend came to India and visited me, I realized she had been thinking about me. I had happy tears in my eyes at that moment.

Jebastin and Vinodh, 2018

May 2019 — Planning Another Trip to India

When I saw an announcement in our church bulletin that another team was being formed to go on a mission trip to India in 2020, my heart skipped a beat. I was surprised to see this, and immediately sent the following text to the contact person:

> India trip... Yes please send more info! - Amy Malay 😊
>
> May 5, 2019

This team was being led by the same ladies that led the trip my sister, Julia, had participated in five years earlier. The team would be visiting and supporting two ministries – Hope Family Home in Kalimpong, and St. Matthew School in Delhi. Yes, I was going to get to meet Sarah Rhakho, the woman "in the trenches" that Julia told us about! I was not familiar with the geography of India yet. When I looked up these two cities on the map, I realized there would not be a practical way to "stop by" in Chennai to meet Jebastin. Yet, somehow, I knew in my heart that I needed to meet him in person.

I kept praying about it and wondering how it would work out. I did not tell Jebastin about the trip at all until about a month later. I did not want him to be disappointed if for some

> *Rejoice in our confident hope. Be patient in trouble and keep on praying.*
>
> Romans 12:12 NLT

reason it did not work out for me to go on the trip. I did not have funds saved up to cover the cost of the trip and had no idea how that would be provided. I was knocking on the doors to see if and how God would open it.

After several informational meetings, I told Jebastin about the *possibility* of me visiting India. I was careful not to make any promises, as much for me as for Jebastin. I was guarding my heart because "what if it doesn't work out?" As more time passed, the dates for the trip were firmed up and the fundraising began. The doors were opening!

Also, my mother, Jo-Ann, felt led to be part of this India trip. She is also part of our Young Living Essential Oils team. Julia's earlier trip and testimony had touched all our hearts, and now since I was planning to go on the trip, our mom was drawn in, too.

We continued to pray about the option to add a week to our trip to visit him. A few weeks later, our team leader, Lena, suggested that perhaps Sarah would accompany us to Chennai. We loved the idea, and once we asked her, Sarah was all in. That settled it. In addition to the other amazing parts of the trip, we were going to spend an extra week with Sarah, visit Chennai, and meet Jebastin!

Shortly after I told him we were coming to Chennai, Jebastin told me he had a girlfriend, Lavanya. Not only that, but they were planning to be married. He even thought maybe the wedding date would be during our visit. How amazing would that be to be there for his wedding!?! He said, "You must be here for my wedding. You are my mom! Without you I cannot start my new life."

> As of the date of this book, the wedding date is still pending due to the Coronavirus pandemic's impact around the world. We are still praying and hoping I can be there to celebrate with Jebastin and Lavanya.

July 2019 – My Mom is Coming to India

During my childhood, every two years or so, other child sponsors would come to visit the Compassion center. They would stay for a whole day and spend a few hours with their sponsored child. That is when I started asking my mom in my letters "when will you come to India?" I even wrote, "My grandmother wants to know when you will come to India."

My question was not answered until mid-2019. My mom told me there was a group from her church coming to India and she might be coming. I remember praying that she would be able to come. A few months later, she sent me the actual dates of the trip. And then, during her flight to India, she texted me, "Tell your grandma that *today* is the day I am coming to India!" What I had prayed about for so long was finally going to happen.

I kept praying about the trip, about our visit, and about my English-speaking skills! I was very nervous about speaking in English. How would we be able to communicate well? I prayed for God to help me.

After that week, I went to soccer practice in the early morning and practiced English with my coach. I am so thankful that God helped me to practice. He truly answered my prayer and during their visit it was not as hard as I thought to speak in English with my mom, grandma Jo-Ann, and Aunt Sarah. I learned to be courageous in speaking English. I learned that it is okay to make mistakes. I learned that it is okay to ask someone to repeat what they said if I did not understand it the first time.

I also thought about how God had a plan all along. If my mom visited India years earlier at the Compassion center, I would only have spent a few hours with her. This visit was going to be a whole week, and I could not wait to meet her.

♥ ♥ ♥

Pause to Ponder

What information have you held back from another person because you wanted to protect them?

What were you protecting that person – or yourself – from?

Describe a time in your life when there were uncertainties and you had to "trust the wait."

♥ ♥ ♥

Noteworthy Notes

Chapter 10

♥

Dream Week

10. Dream Week

The whole week of my mom's visit is imprinted on my mind. I prayed my whole life that I would get to meet her someday. Every moment was so special. From when I saw her to when she had to leave at the end of the week. On the first day of her visit, we went to Women's Christian College (WCC). During my mom's presentation, I sat in the front row as she spoke to about 100 students. I kept wondering, "How did she get to speak here at WCC? She's only been in Chennai for less than one day!" I was amazed that she could do this. Her talk was about "getting past stuck" and how we can learn from our mistakes.

God really blessed our conversations. I tried to listen so carefully to hear the words that were said. It was still difficult to understand. But I learned it is ok to ask for the sentence to be repeated. And we did not make small talk only. God gave me courage to share my testimony and things that were on my heart with my mom and grandma. And they shared some of their testimony with me, too. I always thought that Americans did not have any family problems. But I learned that was not true. I also learned that it is possible to forgive everyone for everything. Because of all we shared with each other, God helped me see that I do not need to be afraid to share my testimony. I realized that my story could plant seeds for Jesus and help others who are like me.

Another highlight of the week was when my mom met my fiancée, Lavanya. We ate a meal together at Lavanya's house, and my mom really surprised me when she used her hands to eat her food like we do in India! But she ate only a small amount of food! I kept saying, "It's not sufficient." Sharing a meal with my mom was another dream I had for a long time. While we were eating together, I was thanking God for another dream come true.

I loved the peppermint essential oil my mom brought along. Every time we were together, I asked if I could use some. It smelled good and felt refreshing on the back of my neck.

I also loved taking my mom for a ride on my motorcycle, and we laughed a lot when she pretended to drive a motorcycle while me and Grandma rode on the back.

When my mom showed me the folder full of the letters I had written to her, my heart and mind were overwhelmed with love. I had happy tears in my eyes. My mom had saved all my letters, and she brought them to Chennai!

Script writing is one of my passions. When God touched my life again, He rebuilt me for doing His work. I tore up my cinematic scripts and prayed for the opportunity to serve God with my writing. The first script I wrote for God is called "Grace Over." God used me for that script, and I learned many things through that experience. That was the first time I saw God working in me and through me.

I wanted to share this part of my life with my mom. So, I asked her to help me write a skit for the youth at my church in English. It was the first time I wrote a script in English. We had so much fun laughing over the pronunciation of some English words as we created the script for that skit! For example, she said "I'll" and I thought she was saying "oil." I was used to British pronunciation, rather than American pronunciation.

I treasured every moment of the week. We had so much fun together, and I cannot stop thinking about all the wonderful memories we created. To this day it makes me feel so happy. The whole week was really a dream come true! I replay the week over and over in my mind and I cannot wait until the next time I can spend more time with my mom and meet the rest of my American family.

Maybe one day we'll find the place where our dreams and reality collide.

There were so many meaningful experiences during the week. The following pages offer a window into the memories created during our six days spent in Chennai.

Day One

The first day was full to the brim! Suresh was our driver again that day. He took us to check in at a women's college. I "unexpectedly" shared a 30-minute talk that day with 100 students. Tthe talk was supposed to have been the next day, but that schedule didn't work, and the principle of the school asked if I could share "now." Since I was intentionally saying "yes" to open doors before me, I said "yes."

We then went to meet Jebastin's fiancée, Lavanya, and her family. We enjoyed a delicious meal at her home, with her family. It was the first meal we ate together with Jebastin. It was also the first meal we ate at someone's home in India. We enjoyed the experience of eating without a table and without utensils.

After visiting there, we went to the beach. We took a four-mile walk along the beach on the Bay of Bengal. We walked and talked and obliged some people on the beach who requested photos with us "foreigners." We joked about how it seemed like we were being followed by paparazzi, and then we chuckled because we realized that Jebastin was not very amused. He did not really want to share us! "Shall we move?" he said. So, we moved on. When we reached the lighthouse, we took the elevator to the top and took in the beautiful views of Chennai.

That evening, we enjoyed dinner with Jebastin's family at his home. We spent valuable time with them in worship, prayer, and fellowship. It was so wonderful to meet and hug the people whose names had been mentioned in Jebastin's letters – his grandma, his sister, and his brother. We also met aunts, uncles, and cousins. It was wonderful to be with them and to see and experience the home where Jebastin lived most of his life.

Day Two

On the second day, Jebastin arranged for us to visit a crocodile park and Mahabalipuram, a monument with huge boulders (the photo used for this book cover was from this monument). We ladies had fun trying to say the name, and Jebastin had just as much fun listening to us pronounce it incorrectly!

We went to another lighthouse – this one had spiral stairs inside, and we climbed to the top. We took a walk on another beach. It was great to see all these sights, but for me, the true highlight was the conversation and relaxed time spent getting to know each other in person.

Day Three

On the third day, I fulfilled a pre-arranged speaking engagement at Vellamal Institute of Technology while Jebastin was working. I felt so honored by this school. They even had signage the size of a mini-billboard created to welcome me. I shared the "getting past stuck" talk there with several hundred students.

That evening, we enjoyed dinner in our hotel room with Jebastin and Lavanya. Later that night, we visited the church Jebastin attends for night prayer (10 pm to 12:30 am). It was a blessed time of worship and prayer in the presence of the Holy Spirit. After the prayer time, I was invited to share. I gave a brief testimony of God's faithfulness to encourage those gathered. Fellowship and snacks followed. I loved seeing how Jebastin is surrounded by devoted Christ-followers that support and encourage him in his faith journey.

Day Four

It had been a late night, and on the fourth day, we three ladies had a long overdue "day of rest" in our hotel room. After a leisurely breakfast, Sarah said to me, "Amy, you need to write all this down." She had been noticing all the amazing ways God was working in our hearts and lives. She could tell many pieces of a "puzzle" were becoming known. I had been noticing it, too, and as soon as Sarah said the words, there was a quickening in my spirit. I knew that THIS was the book I was to write. I had always known I would write a book someday. And someday had arrived! I spent most of the morning writing. It was like the Lord just poured it out through my heart and mind and fingertips onto my computer screen.

By the time Jebastin joined us later that afternoon, I had written a basic outline in a Q&A style format so that Jebastin and I could each answer the questions and tell our story from two perspectives. I told him about it, saying, "Guess what? We are going to write a book!" He just grinned and said, "Ok mom!"

And so we sat and talked about the book. I asked questions and He answered. As he told me his story, I typed it, and our book became a real thing.

We also looked through and sorted all the letters that Jebastin had written to me over the years. He loved seeing them and reminiscing over the pictures he drew. They provided a great reference point for us as we put together the timeline of our memories.

As we were chatting, Jebastin asked me, "Will you help me find a child to sponsor?" My heart melted. The realization of the impact that my sponsorship had on his life was overwhelming. We looked at the Compassion website a little bit that day and decided to follow-up again later to get the child sponsorship started.

That evening, Jebastin's friend Karthick joined us. We had a fun time chatting and then laughing about the English phrase, "sounds good," which I say frequently. They found it funny since it has nothing to do with actual sound. We took a metro ride to visit a mall. We enjoyed walking around, and we had dinner there. We took photos and, again, we simply enjoyed each other's company.

Day Five

The fifth day was Sunday. We traveled about an hour to a village church where Jebastin's uncle is the Pastor.

The bus ride was fun and worship-filled, regardless of the traffic jam we encountered. We arrived an hour later than expected, and the congregation simply waited for us.

When we arrived, the service started. I was honored to share a message about faith and faithfulness with those gathered that day, with translation by Jebastin's uncle.

After the service, we enjoyed a prayer time. A highlight for me was praying for Jebastin in person. We spent almost 20 years praying for each other from afar. It was so special to pray together in person multiple times throughout the week.

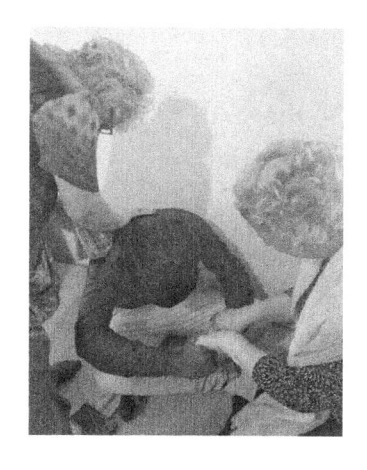

We also enjoyed a meal that had been prepared for us. I will never forget the way Jebastin kept sneaking more rice onto my banana leaf plate when I was not looking. He told me the meal was made especially for us and that we needed to eat all the food on our plate.

Well, I was eating a lot and kept thinking how the pile of rice was not getting any smaller. I finally finished it, and I was SOOO full. Later, I realized how he had tricked me, and thought, "that is just like a son, to tease his mother."

Day Six

On the sixth day, our last day in Chennai, we rested and packed our things so they would be ready for our early morning flight. In the evening, Jebastin, Suresh, and Karthick took us around town to do some shopping.

Part of the shopping we did was for a sari blouse for me. The "pre-made" blouses were not available in my size. I already knew that Jebastin was not one to give up easily. For this mission, he found a shop keeper that agreed to measure me and make the sari blouse in just one hour since we were leaving the next morning.

The measurements were taken, and then we all went for dinner. At that meal, we found out there is such a thing as "too spicy" for Jebastin. I thought the food we were eating was VERY spicy. I thought it was just me until he said he thought it was spicy, too. I was relieved since my mouth was on fire, even though we had ordered it "mild."

Another fun memory while walking was the traffic and how we crossed the street. We would line up sideways next to each other. When Jebastin would start moving in between motorcycles and cars and trucks whizzing behind us and in front of us, we would "just go" even if it did not seem like it was clear. Somehow, we made it safely every time.

We went back to the sari shop and waited for the sari blouse to be completed. Then Karthick, Jebastin and I walked back to the hotel, while Suresh gave a motorcycle ride back to my mom and Sarah. We closed the night with worship and prayer before saying good night to Suresh and Karthick.

Before Jebastin left for the night, we gave him some gifts for himself and some crafts he could use with the children at his church. We also gave him some of the essential oils we had with us, including the peppermint he loved so much!

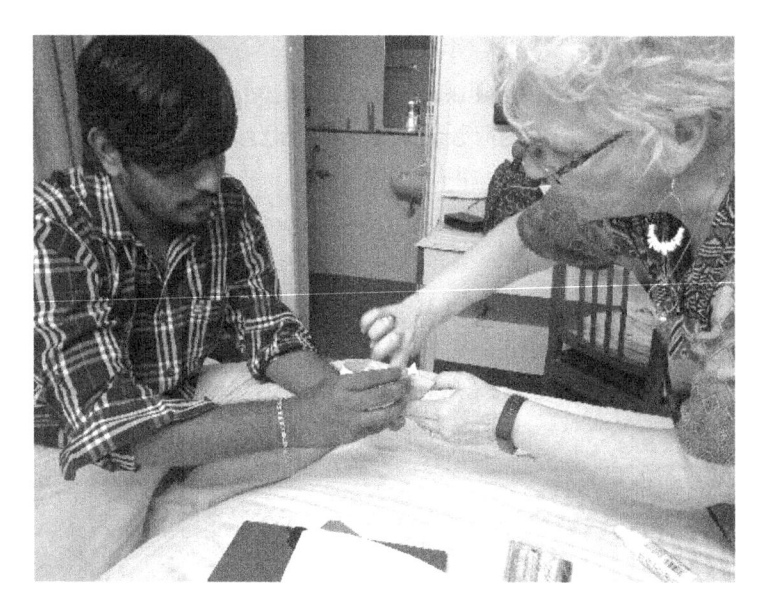

♥ ♥ ♥

Pause to Ponder

Describe a time when you had a conversation that was "blessed."

What made that conversation meaningful to you?

How often do you tease or joke around with those you love?

What is a fun memory that brings joy to your heart every time you think of it?

♥ ♥ ♥

Noteworthy Notes

Chapter 11

♥

Goodbye... For Now

11. Goodbye... For Now

The week was so full of blessings. So full of remembering and making new memories. So full of love and joy and hugs and tears. It was truly a "dream week" and none of us wanted it to end. But it did.

On the morning of the seventh day, we woke up at 4 am to travel to the airport. The day for "goodbye" had arrived. It was a difficult morning for all of us. Jebastin and Karthick accompanied us. We walked to the subway station and took the subway to the airport. There was some small talk, but mostly we just took in as many smiles and hugs as possible in the last moments we were together.

The goodbyes were difficult for me. I held back my tears until the airplane took off. I had received such a special gift – an answer to prayers I had prayed for so long.

> *Whatever is good and perfect is a gift coming down to us from God our Father, who created all the lights in the heavens…*
>
> James 1:17 NLT

The week spent getting to know each other in-person had raised my awareness of our connection. Our bond deepened to a point I never thought possible. Saying goodbye felt like letting it go – again.

I am full to the brim with love for my son, and my eyes seem to overflow with tears when I think about the physical distance between us and the amount of time that might go by before we can spend time together again.

The mother-son bond the Lord created between us cannot be broken. Our hearts are forever connected, and when we do meet in person again, it will be a joyful occasion. So, stay tuned for updates on that! Because, you know, He NEVER stops working!

♥ ♥ ♥

Pause to Ponder

Who or what have you said
goodbye to in the past?

What helps to remind you of God's
good and perfect plans?

What are some ways that you "close the distance"
between yourself and loved ones who are far away?

♥ ♥ ♥

Noteworthy Notes

Chapter 12

♥

Leftover Baskets of Provision

12. Leftover Baskets of Provision

Since meeting Jebastin in person and hearing more of his life story, I have thought, "Why didn't I do more to connect with him before?" Maybe I could have written more letters. Maybe I could have shared more of my life with him through the letters. Maybe I could have visited India sooner. I started to feel guilty, inadequate, and unworthy of the love and honor bestowed on me as his mom.

I have come to realize, though, that these feelings are not the truth. The truth is found in what Jebastin says often: "God has a plan for everything." I already knew this, but Jebastin's unquestioning faith in God's plan and timing was and is a good reminder to me.

It has inspired me to stop questioning why things happened the way they did, or in

> Send the crowds away so they can go to the villages and buy food for themselves." But Jesus said, "That isn't necessary – you feed them."
> "But we have only five loaves of bread and two fish!" they answered. "Bring them here," he said. Then he told the people to sit down on the grass. Jesus took the five loaves and two fish, looked up to heaven, and blessed them. Then, breaking the loaves into pieces, he gave the bread to the disciples, who distributed it to the people. They all ate as much as they wanted, and afterward, the disciples picked up twelve baskets of leftovers.
>
> Matthew 14:15-20 NLT

the timing they did, or why some things did not happen. Instead, I can simply trust that it was His plan. It was His perfect timing, His perfect way, and His perfect love.

Like the young boy in the book of Matthew, I had given my "fishes and loaves," and the Lord multiplied them for His plan and His purpose. I did what I could, given the circumstances in my life at the time.

God did what I could not do. He took my efforts and compounded them. He used me to impact Jebastin's life more than I could have imagined. He is using Jebastin to impact my life more than he ever thought was possible.

> The Lord says, "I will give you back what you lost to the swarming locusts..."
>
> Joel 2.25 NLT

We are still collecting the leftover baskets of His provision for our lives and learning how to share them with others. He was working. He is still working – truly restoring the years lost to the locusts – in simple ways and in profound ways.

The day after my mom left Chennai, I had a job interview. God is continuing to use me through my work. I was offered the new job as an accountant at Christian Missions Charitable Trust (CMCT).

A few months earlier, I prayed and asked God to help me find a job with better pay. Not long after that, I was at the CMCT office. CMCT is a client of my former employer. While we were talking, the CMCT contact person asked me if I would come and work for their ministry.

I spoke with my former employer and soon it was all arranged. I started that job in June 2020. I am excited for the opportunity to get experience serving with a Christian ministry. God has a plan and He is using me!

♥ ♥ ♥

Pause to Ponder

What lies have you believed?

How did you eventually recognize the truth?

What represents the leftover
fishes and loaves in your life?

How do you see God using your gifts?

♥ ♥ ♥

Noteworthy Notes

Chapter 13

♥

Staying Connected

13. Staying Connected

Our God closes the distance gap. Physical distance cannot prevent or remove our heart connection. These days there are so many apps and technology options. They are a blessing to help us stay connected. And connected we are! We check in with each other frequently. Even this makes me chuckle at the fun God must have had working out this plan. You see, I have always been one who "checks in" with my husband when I am out and about. We have joked about it many times.

And now, I have a son on the other side of the globe who "checks in" to make sure I have eaten enough and slept enough and arrived on schedule to various activities. I cannot hold back my smile when I see a "check-in" text from Jebastin. "What are you doing mom?" "Where are you mom?" "What about your lunch mom?" "Mom you are still awake!?" or "Love you mom."

Even Jebastin's frequency of calling me mom is a God-wink. For all the years no one called me mom, now I have a son who calls me mom with every sentence, because that is how it is done in his culture. I never knew this kind of love before. The protective and caring love of a son for his mom.

During one conversation, I asked Jebastin more about why he did not have a last name. He had previously showed me his ID which lists only "Jebastin." I was trying to understand this since it is not the custom in the United

States. During my trip to India, there were other individuals I met who also did not use a last name. And then I was wondering… and so I asked, "Would you like to use our last name?" His response was, "Yea… Mom. I would love it…" It was another heart connection, and he began informally using the name Jebastin J. Malay.

A few weeks later, we also connected through child sponsorship. I recalled Jebastin's request for me to help him find a child to sponsor. I thought about the two young girls I am sponsoring – "Any" from Columbia and "Konjit" from Ethiopia. The Lord impressed upon me the idea to share in the sponsorship and letter-writing for the girls. I shared the idea with Jebastin, and he loved it. He wrote letters to them right away. He calls them his "princess sisters."

One week was not enough time to spend with my mom. I missed her so much when she left Chennai and I still miss her every day. I am thankful to God that we can connect on Facebook, Instagram, WhatsApp, Zoom, YouVersion Bible app, MapMyWalk, and Marco Polo. We also share some files on Google Drive. Whatever options are available, I will connect with my mom!

Almost every day we talk by phone or video. We text each other throughout each day. I get a big smile on my face every time I see a "good morning" or a "good night" message from my mom. We are also working together on projects like this book and some videos. I love writing to my princess sisters Any and Konjit through Compassion. And I am even using the family name of Malay.

All these connections make me so happy. We study the Word of God together and pray for each other and our family in the US and India. I love to see photos of my mom's meals. We sometimes even eat "virtual meals" together. India time is nine and a half hours ahead of Pennsylvania time, so she eats her lunch while I eat my dinner and we talk about the day!

I never felt a mother's love like this before in my life. Even when I was young and my birth mother was alive, I was not old enough to understand or realize that kind of love. And by God's grace, I now have that love through my mom, Amy.

♥ ♥ ♥

Pause to Ponder

What God-winks have you noticed lately?

How often do you usually "check-in" with loved ones?

How often do you tell your loved ones that you love them?

How often is often enough?

♥ ♥ ♥

Noteworthy Notes

Chapter 14

♥

It's the Little Things

14. It's the Little Things...

As I spent time with Jebastin in Chennai, and as we shared phone and video conversations after I was back in the US, we became more and more aware of the many "little things" we had in common.

While each similarity is not that significant on its own, each new awareness compounded the point I think God was trying to make in our hearts.

> While visiting with Jebastin's family, I found out that he is a fourth-generation believer in his family. So am I.

> We both frequently use the phrase, "by the grace of God."

> We both know many people yet have a few close friends.

> We both love nature photography.

> We both smile and smile big. A LOT!

> We are both employed by multiple businesses. We are also both self-employed.

> We both have big, God-given dreams and goals.

> We both enjoy writing.

I remember chuckling and thinking at one point, "Ok, Lord, you're just showing off now!"

And then in the next moment, I could hardly believe I was not dreaming.

He had a faithful and purposeful plan. The plan He had been working out all along. The plan where He had chosen us specifically for each other.

> While on a video call with Jebastin, I noticed he was twirling his hair. I twirl my hair the same way.

> On a video chat, I noticed Jebastin has a scar on the hairline on his forehead. And so do I.

> When I received an email from Jebastin, I noticed he used the middle initial "J." So do I.

> FAMILY is a top priority in both our lives.

> Jebastin has had a dream to visit Thailand since he was 18. I went to Thailand when he was about 3 years old and would love to go back someday.

> In 1995, the year Jebastin was born, I named a stuffed bear "Benjamin." I intended to use this name for a son, when and if I had one. This is the name Jebastin chose for himself when he was baptized at age 18.

> We both wanted to be missionaries.

> We both have a great sense of humor.

> Peppermint is my favorite essential oil. While we were visiting Chennai, Jebastin tried peppermint. He asked several times each day if he could have more peppermint. I think he loves it, too!

> Did I mention our big smiles?

I truly believe there are no coincidences when it comes to the faithful working of God in our lives.

> Consistent is a word that others have used to describe each of us.

Quite a few tears of overwhelming
joy and wonder appeared
out of nowhere
as God repeatedly
made me aware
that **I was the mom**
He had chosen for Jebastin.

> We both took piano lessons earlier in life, but did not continue...

That though I had not raised
him in my home,
I had raised him in my heart.

> We both recommitted our lives to Christ at age 22.

With each new day,
this reality continues to sink into
my heart and mind.

> We both majored in accounting in college.

183

I found this quote while in India. It is a meaningful explanation and reflection on the big smiles we have in common, regardless of the challenges of the past, present, or future.

Just because a person smiles all the time,
doesn't mean their life is perfect.
The smile is a symbol of HOPE and STRENGTH.

♥ ♥ ♥

Pause to Ponder

Do you believe in coincidences? Why or why not?

Describe a time when you noticed
God's sense of humor.

When were you able to smile in spite of something
difficult happening in your life?

♥ ♥ ♥

Noteworthy Notes

Chapter 15

♥

Learning to Turn

15. Learning to Turn

This book has been a way to share with others some of the trauma and healing we have experienced. Trauma is defined as a deeply distressing or disturbing experience. As humans, we all experience trauma as we journey through life. And we wanted to share not only the trauma, but what helped us – and still helps us – to overcome trauma and find places of freedom and healing.

Throughout my life, I have learned to turn in certain ways that helped me to thrive and not just survive. First and foremost, I turn toward Jesus. Like the well-known hymn lyrics:

Turn your eyes upon Jesus
Look full in His wonderful face
And the things of earth will grow strangely dim
In the light of His glory and grace

Jesus is truly the best leader and example for me to learn from and model after. But how do we do the work of "turning?" I have found there are three specific actions I can take to help me turn toward Him in times when life feels like a struggle.

   1. **Reading the Word** – The Bible, the Word of God, is THE source of truth and hope in my life. Spending time reading it, studying it, speaking it out loud, and reflecting on it have been invaluable for me as

I strive to turn toward and stand firm on His promises. Biblical affirmation statements have been key to the process of transforming my mind. I specifically

> ... let God transform you into a new person by changing the way you think. Then you will learn to know God's will for you, which is good and pleasing and perfect.
>
> Romans 12:2 NLT

love using "I AM" statements to remind myself of the truths of God's Word. For example:

I AM a vessel of God's love and grace to others.
I AM a beloved child of the King of Kings.
I AM resourced by The Source of life and love.
I AM healed and free because of the price HE paid for me.

2. **Worship** – Worship music speaks to my heart and helps me to turn my spirit toward Jesus. I have found it is the quickest way for me to change my perspective on any situation I face in life. See the "Helpful Resources" section to see some of our favorite worship songs.

3. **Prayer** – Both speaking and listening are part of good communication, and the same can be said of prayer – our communication with God. He wants to hear from us, and he also wants us to turn our ears toward Him – to listen for His voice. He does

not hide His wisdom from us. In fact, in Proverbs 1 we read that wisdom is calling out to us.

Throughout my life, when I faced difficult times, I would always talk with God in my heart, like He is my friend. I was always asking, "Why did you do this to me?" or "Why did this happen?"

> *Wisdom shouts in the streets. She cries out in the public square. She calls to the crowds along the main street, to those gathered in front of the city gate.*
>
> Proverbs 1:20-21 NLT

Many times, when I am reading my Bible, an answer would come to me. And I was reassured that God has a plan for everything. So, I just kept waiting to see His plan. He is a faithful and true friend. This kind of friend never disappoints me, and I do not want to disappoint Him either.

♥ ♥ ♥

Pause to Ponder

What causes you to turn toward the Lord?

What is a Biblical affirmation statement you could use to transform the way you think?

♥ ♥ ♥

Noteworthy Notes

Chapter 16

♥

Meaningful Words

16. Meaningful Words

In addition to Biblical affirmation statements, I have been prayerfully choosing a word of the year since 2017. The word I chose that first year was TRANSFORMATION.

In hindsight, that year proved to be a very significant year of transformation in my life. I also now know that this was the year that Jebastin recommitted his life to Christ and experienced profound spiritual transformation. Perhaps I was guided to this word that year, not only for me, but also for the son I had lost touch with and who was experiencing struggles on his journey.

My word for 2020 is IMPACT. I chose this word because I want to give intentional focus on making a difference as I serve others. It is the Lord, working in me and through me, that has truly made the difference.

The second half of 2020 has just begun. God has helped me to impact lives and my life has been impacted. It is so true that when we serve, we are in turn served. Though I went on the trip to India to minister to others, I was also ministered to by many. Though I have made the effort to write this book as a ministry to others, I have been ministered to through this process.

My mom encouraged me to choose a word of the year before she came to visit me in India. The word I chose for 2020 is FAITHFUL. I chose this word to remind me of God's faithfulness to me, even when I was not faithful to Him. I am grateful for his grace and love in my life. This year, one of the dreams of my life came true. I got to meet my mom in person!

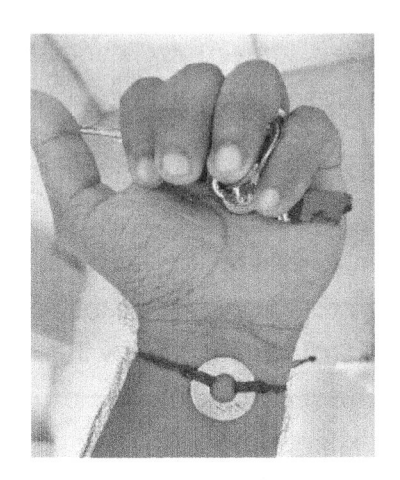

The Lord has shown His faithfulness in both our lives. As I continue to offer my abilities and my testimony to Him, I see His faithfulness in using me to serve Him. I see this even with the small business I recently started so that I could serve Him by doing accounting work for ministries.

One of the names of God is El Hanne'eman, The Faithful God. He is not just faithful—He is relentlessly powerful in His faithfulness. Nothing can keep Him from being faithful to His children. He has more than good intentions. He will remain faithful forever.

♥ ♥ ♥

Pause to Ponder

Have you ever picked a "word of the year"?

What is a one-word theme in your life this year?

♥ ♥ ♥

Noteworthy Notes

Chapter 17

♥

The Power of Testimonies

17. The Power of Testimonies

My heart is still full and overflowing with the blessings the Lord poured into my life during the week I spent with Jebastin in Chennai. During the week, I was awakened to the work our God accomplishes through us and in us. Over all the years we had been writing to each other, He had been working. The resulting bond between us was and is more than I could ever ask or imagine. I realized during a conversation with a friend that what I was just noticing now actually represented a lifetime of God working it all out. My new awareness was backed by years of faithful prayer – my prayers and the prayers of many others. And by the grace of God, dreams became reality.

> *Now all glory to God, who is able, through his mighty power at work within us, to accomplish infinitely more than we might ask or think.*
>
> Ephesians 3:20 NLT

Several times during the week, Jebastin and I shared with each other testimonies of God's transforming power, healing, and faithfulness in our lives. During one of our walks, Jebastin shared how he had turned away from God after we lost touch. And how God touched his life again and how he thought to search for me only after he had turned back to God.

I also took the opportunity to share some of my testimony with him. I shared some of the difficult times in my life that I had not shared with him in letters when he was a child. He looked at me in amazement and said, "How did you do this?" My response? "By God's grace."

"I always thought you never had any real problems in your life," he said. "Why didn't you ever tell me about these things? I am your son!"

I think that was the moment when this truth plunged into my heart like an arrow: *He had truly counted himself as my son all along. I just had not seen it.* It was like my eyes – and the eyes of my heart had been blinded. All the sudden, Jebastin's questions caused the blindfold to be taken away so I could see the truth.

It was overwhelming. I was not even sure what to do or say about it at that moment. But one thing I did know: He needed to hear ALL my testimony. There was not time to share it all during the week of our visit, but I told him there was more and that I would share it with him.

Once I was back in Pennsylvania, I followed through. I took time to write out my life story, and then I sent it to him by email. I wanted him to know all the ways God has been faithful in my life. We talked about it on the phone after he read it. It was a meaningful conversation and provided more opportunity for us to connect with each other.

The answers to some of the questions I previously had started to become clear in my mind. The answer was in the testimony of God's faithfulness in my life. THAT is the legacy I want to leave. A legacy of standing firm on His promises. For others to know just how faithful God was in my life, I needed to share the hardest parts of my story.

Now, I am embracing the opportunity to share as many of my life experiences - past and present - as I can with my son. I have shared parts of my testimony in different settings, before and after my trip to India. I

> *Let each generation tell its children of your mighty acts; let them proclaim your power.*
>
> Psalm 145:4 NLT

now share some of my "early years" testimony within the context of this story. My desire is for this story – this entire book – to be a seed of hope.

May you be encouraged by God's faithfulness in my life and know that He is just as faithful in your life. He truly never stops working. He truly uses EVERY experience to bring good (in the end) out of the sorrows we experience in our earthly lives, even if we cannot understand it at the time. Because of His grace, I am "more than okay" despite difficult circumstances. I am thriving and not just surviving.

Amy's Earlier Testimony

I remember my mom taking me and my younger sister to a weekly church club for girls. At the club, we would participate in crafts and learn about Jesus. We went to the Sunday services at that church, too. I remember asking Jesus into my heart and saying yes to being baptized

> They have defeated him by the blood of the Lamb and by their testimony…
>
> Revelation 12:11a NLT

when I was 8 years old. I remember standing there in the pool of water with the pastor and telling all who had gathered that I had accepted Jesus into my heart and wanted to live for Him. After the pastor baptized me, I walked up out of the pool, knowing that I was a child of God.

My childhood was not without hurts, and my faith in Jesus helped me cope with those. There was sexual abuse inflicted by my grandfather in my very early years. Though I did not know it at the time, I was one of many who experienced abuse from him. This all came to light much later when I was in 9th or 10th grade. By then, my grandfather had died. Before he died, when I was in 8th grade, I remember intentionally forgiving him while he came to stay at our home during his terminal illness. I believe this forgiveness was only by God's grace. The Holy Spirit gave me the ability to comprehend what I was doing.

Also, during my earlier childhood days, my parents separated multiple times, and there were multiple housing and school changes - at least eight or nine school changes prior to high school. I was extremely shy at the time and these changes caused quite a bit of anxiety for me. I remember an awful feeling of dread each time I was taken into a full classroom of students and introduced as the "new student who was joining the class today." Again, by God's grace, I always found a good friend or two in each new class.

Between my 6th and 7th grade year, my parents divorced. About two years later, my mother remarried, and blended family life began.

Along with that came another move between my 8th and 9th grade years. I recall this move as the most devastating to me. I had been at one school for two and a half years, the longest I recall to that point. I had a best friend and other friends. I had "settled in" so to speak. I remember praying and pleading for there to be a way for me to stay at that school. But it was not to be. By God's grace, I again made new friends and settled in at the new school. I was able to stay at that school for four years until I graduated.

Somewhere during those four years of high school, I went astray from following God. I did not stay true to God's plan for my life. I was in an inappropriate relationship with a boyfriend. Only later during my college years did that relationship end – and with no small amount of heartache. Shortly after that breakup, I recommitted my life to Christ. I was 22 years old at that time. Jehovah Rophe, the God who heals, made it possible for me to *find healing from some of the hurts of the past through my growing relationship with Him.*

This came over time. Journaling, prayer, worship, and other spiritual growth disciplines were essential in the healing process. I know that working at the missionary agency, along with the discipleship experiences I had in preparation for mission work, and continued discipleship during various mission trips were key for my healing journey.

My journey of healing continues, even to this day! Since my childhood, I have known God is present in my life. During some of the struggles I experienced, God's grace was my lifeline. Yet, I still remember moments where I would wonder why He was not "moving the mountain."

Looking back, I know He WAS moving. He was also standing with me in the struggle. He was the reason I could stand firm. And when I could not stand, He was there to catch me, to uphold me with His righteous right hand.

> But the Lord stood at my side and gave me strength…
>
> 2 Timothy 4:17 NLT

♥ ♥ ♥

Pause to Ponder

What part of your testimony have you
hesitated to share with others?

Why do you think you hesitated?

Think of one person that could be encouraged
by part of your story.

How and when might you share
that part of your story with them?

♥ ♥ ♥

Noteworthy Notes

♥

Our Great Cloud of Witnesses

♥

Our Great Cloud of Witnesses

On this journey, we have been surrounded by a "great cloud of witnesses," the one in heaven, and the family and friends who have watched all or part of our journey unfold. They have been cheering us on, perhaps laughing or crying with us, and sometimes running the race right beside us.

We both have large families, and so these pages do not include everyone, but only a small sample of those who have been part of our support system along the way. May these additional shared testimonies of God's faithful work in our lives point to the way He has worked to not only impact our lives – but also the lives of others around us.

> *Therefore, since we are surrounded by such a huge cloud of witnesses... let us strip off every weight that slows us down, especially the sin that so easily trips us up. And let us run with endurance the race God has set before us. We do this by keeping our eyes on Jesus, the champion who initiates and perfects our faith.*
>
> Hebrews 12:1-2

♥ ♥ ♥

Jo-Ann, Amy's mother

I have tears of joy as emotions surface. I am remembering all the years of praying from my heart to God for a child for my daughter Amy. As the end of her childbearing years approached, my prayers changed to a "miracle" child. I clung to the story of Sarah, the Bible character who bore a son in her later years. I affirmed that God is all powerful, all knowing and ever present. Not long ago, I assured Amy that she was not 99 yet!

I looked forward to meeting her Compassion child while we were on a mission trip to India. His picture had been on her bathroom mirror and on her refrigerator. When I inquired, she spoke of the Compassion program and of how she prayed for him. They had lost contact and she was excited when she reported that he had found her on Facebook, and they were communicating once again.

I am not sure of the exact moment that I realized that Jebastin was *THE child* that I had been praying for. God had answered my prayers before I even prayed them!! Maybe it was when I saw them in deep conversation while walking on the beach, or maybe when he began calling me "Grandma." I kept thinking of the verse in the book of Joel about the Lord restoring the years the locusts have eaten.

When I arrived at the late-night prayer meeting at Jebastin's church, I noticed part of that verse on a sign.

I was affirmed. I knew for sure that I was there in India to witness the mother and son bonding and to see first-hand the answers to my prayers over the years. I am praising God for His love, affirmation, and goodness!

Hallelujah! AMEN!

♥ ♥ ♥

Ron, Amy's stepfather

I met Amy when she was 12 years old. When her mother and father divorced, she was a big support to her mother in helping with the younger children. She was the oldest and a mother figure to her younger siblings. When I married her mother, this was, of course, another big change.

She accepted all these changes. She was very quiet and did not like to have her picture taken. She had a good sense of humor. She cared about and helped others. She felt strongly about people being treated fairly. She always did well in school and thrived in her education. At age 14, she helped her mother and I run a pet store. She even managed the store while her baby sister, Julia, was born the following year.

Later, there were challenges she faced, and she overcame those, too. The tragedies in her life have given her a tremendous compassion and wisdom for helping and supporting others. She has insight that many others do not have because of her life experiences. She has found a way (through Jesus!) to rise to the challenge of the "hand she's been dealt."

When she joined The John Maxwell Team, I noticed how she dug into studying and growing to become the person she is now. We could tell she was changing and growing. She no longer had a problem with having her picture taken.

She is now comfortable in her own skin and she is sharing more of who she really is. Recently, she shared part of her story on a local radio station. She sounded so professional and it made me realize just how much of a new creation she is! Amy's story is the testimony of someone who is realizing and becoming who she really is in Christ.

During Amy and Jo-Ann's trip to India, I looked forward to their daily updates. Amy posted pictures, and Jo-Ann would add comments later to help explain the experiences represented by the pictures. During the last part of the trip, when they met Jebastin, I noticed a steady stream of personal affirmations and little miracles along the way. It was obvious to me that God had orchestrated a spiritual journey above and beyond what had been planned.

While still in India, Amy added Jebastin to our private family Facebook group. She shared a post to welcome him, and in that post, he called me Grandpa. In another comment, Amy shared a photo that included two snapshots - one of Jebastin as a child and one of the two of them together on the trip. She said, "Jeba, you still have the same great smile." and he commented back, "A smile like my mom's." I realized after a few minutes that by "my mom's" he meant *like Amy's* smile! I was amazed to realize that Jebastin had truly claimed us all as his family. And just like that, we had another member of the family - another grandson, nephew, and cousin - Amy's son.

♥ ♥ ♥

Patrick, Amy's husband

I met Amy when we were both at YWAM St Croix. She was the driver of the van that picked me up from the airport when I arrived in September 1997. Some time went by, and I learned to know her better. I realized she was "my girl." When we shared testimonies... hers included some hard things. I thought it must have been hard for her to share that with the group... I invited her to sit and talk one day and it turned into a five-hour talk. We talked about everything in life and had a lot in common. We both wanted to have a family and a lot of kids, and most of all we both wanted to live for God and serve in missions. More than ever, I felt she was the girl for me from God.

After we had been married for quite a few years, and no kids came along... we both figured if it were God's plan, he would give us kids. We did not talk about it very much. But I knew it was something Amy still wanted. As time went by, nieces and nephews came along. And then more nieces and nephews. I asked Amy if it bothered her that we did not have kids. She said she was sometimes sad about it, but also that she was trusting God's plan for our lives.

Jebastin was the "refrigerator kid" for a long time. We received pictures and letters from him. Amy would always read the letters to me. We could tell he was smart and did well in his studies. We prayed for him.

It was exciting when Amy said Jebastin found her on Facebook. I thought it was great because we thought we would never hear from him again after the Compassion center closed. And I also remember the day Amy told me that he wanted to call her mom. I could tell that it meant a lot to her.

Later, when the trip to India became an opportunity, I could hardly believe she would be meeting him. I did not realize how much of a connection there would be. But when she came back from the trip, I realized that Jebastin was no longer the "refrigerator kid." Now he was officially part of the family. His personality is fun-loving, and I can tell he loves us a lot. He has brought a lot joy to Amy's heart, and mine too. I look forward to the day when I can meet him in person.

♥ ♥ ♥

Rebecca, Amy's sister

Since Amy was just 27 months old, she has been a motherly figure in my life. I am sure she helped take care of me through my infant and toddler years. I remember playing horses and Barbies together; Mowing and driving together; Watching our younger siblings together. She was always there – my sister, my friend.

Adulthood came. We both married and were each other's maid of honor! In my mind and dreams we would raise our families together. This is where our lives made more of a separation as Amy was focused on a life of mission trips with her husband and I was a farmer's wife raising little farmers. We stayed in touch with phone calls and visits. She never missed a birthday or anniversary! She was always there – my sister, my friend.

When she moved back to the same town as me, I thought we would spend so much more time together. But the differences in our lives and schedules did not allow for that. So, we scheduled monthly lunch dates to catch up. Last year, during one of these lunch dates she told me Jebastin had found her on Facebook. We had not spoken a lot over the years about our Compassion children. We both knew we had them. It was so neat that he had searched her out and found her – his mom.

All this time we were simultaneously mothering together! Hers was through letters, prayers, and pictures. Mine was more hands-on, but also included lots of prayers and pictures! My dream of raising our kids together actually happened and we had not been aware of it until Amy went to visit Jebastin in India. The awareness that she was his mother and he was her son was awakened!

Amy at her core is a faithful person. Always loving God, loving others, and growing in Christ. Always there – my sister, my friend, a mother.

♥ ♥ ♥

Julia, Amy's sister

When my oldest sister, Amy, climbed into my car because our parking lot conversation was getting too cold and too long to continue outside, the words of Psalm 47:2 ran through my mind.

> *For the Lord Most High is awesome. He is the great King of all the earth.*
>
> Psalm 47:2

She was telling me about her son, Jebastin. HER SON. When Amy tells me about Jebastin, things about his personality and his skill set. He reminds me of HER! God ordained her to be Jebastin's adoptive mother from the other side of the world. He chose for her a son that she would have things in common with. And I kept thinking, "how awesome is our God!"

We sat in a car much like this one several years earlier and cried together tears over the children she never had. It was not something we talked of often, but when we did there were tears. But God had given her a child. She had a child all this time, and she did not know he needed her as a mom just as much as she needed him as a son.

One word that describes Amy is "consistent." Another friend of ours has referred to her as "like the ocean". She is calming, dependable, and consistent. Consistently over many years she wrote letters and sent money. Maybe at times she could barely afford her discipline of tithing and yet her core values kept her consistently writing and contributing.

And now, in February 2020, she has met the son she always had but did not know. How awesome is our God most high! He is always working in ways we would not expect. He answers our prayers in His own fashion and in His own timing.

♥ ♥ ♥

Debby, Amy's friend since grade 6

The first time Amy talked about going to India to meet Jebastin, she told me that if it were meant to be, God would provide a way to make it happen. The idea of her meeting the child whose photo hung on her refrigerator for years seemed like just that - an idea.

But God was at work!

A couple of weeks later Amy said to me, "Hey there is a mission trip being planned to India with some people from my church." She did not know for sure if the trip would be in the area where Jebastin lives. "But wouldn't it be cool if it worked out that I could go? And wouldn't it be even cooler if Jebastin and I got to meet?!" God continued to work.

The fundraising began and the details of the trip fell into place. Still to this day, I am amazed to see how God orchestrated every detail of the trip so that Amy was able to meet her son, Jebastin.

♥ ♥ ♥

Sherrie, Amy's friend and colleague

This story reminds us to rely on God's Sovereignty. I have worked with Amy for four years. Somewhere along the way, we discovered that we both support children through Compassion International. In early 2018, she shared with me that her Compassion child, Jebastin, searched for and found her on Facebook. She had sponsored him for many years, but lost touch when the Compassion center in his area closed.

In the spring of 2019, Amy told me about the possible trip to India, and how she hoped to meet Jebastin while she was there. The mission trip was still a long way off, and many were praying for doors to open. Time went by, the needed funds were raised, the details were worked out, and the excitement continued to build. There were three parts to the trip, and the third part was where she would get to meet Jebastin.

I could sense the joy in her heart during all the parts of the trip, and I could tell the meeting with Jebastin was super special. It was clear that the time spent together produced a whole new level of connection. AMAZING God things were happening! The day that Amy traveled home, I said to my husband, "I think that since Amy never had children of her own, connecting with Jebastin has awakened areas of her life that she could never have comprehended."

Since Amy's return home, joy exudes from her - above and beyond her usual calm, positive, and lovely character. The stories that she has shared with me are both heart wrenching and heartwarming.

Amy and Jebastin have both experienced a great deal of struggle in their lives – on opposite sides of the planet. Yet, God wove together this relationship without either of them realizing how profound the impact would be. The connection is unmistakably God's hand at work. As you have read about their story, I encourage you to fully trust in God's Sovereignty.

> *For I know the plans I have for you, says the Lord, plans for good and not for disaster, to give you a future and a hope.*
>
> Jeremiah 29:11 NLT

♥ ♥ ♥

Sarah, Amy's friend and Executive Director of St. Matthew School, Delhi, India

Sister Lena Arbogast sent me an email asking me if I would like to go to Chennai with Sister Amy Malay and her mother, Jo-Ann Kreider. Right away I said "yes," and I was overwhelmed with thanks to have the opportunity to go with them. God is so faithful and so wonderful. As it says in Isaiah 55, we cannot fathom His plans.

When we arrived in Chennai, I met Jebastin, whom Sister Amy had sponsored for almost 20 years. He was waiting for his mother with beautiful flowers in his hands. At that moment, I felt God's amazing love. It was so touching to see how God brought them together and to see the wonderful and amazing work of our Lord in Sister Amy and in her son's life.

I could see God's words being fulfilled in their lives. All the way from the US to India, how

> *"My thoughts are nothing like your thoughts," says the Lord. "And my ways are far beyond anything you could imagine. For just as the heavens are higher than the earth, so my ways are higher than your ways and my thoughts higher than your thoughts. The rain and the snow come down from the heavens and stay on the ground to water the earth. They cause the grain to grow, producing seed for the farmer and bread for the hungry. It is the same with my word. I send it out, and it always produces fruit. It will accomplish all I want it to, and it will prosper everwhere I send it..*
>
> Isaiah 55:8-11

God connected them is just beyond imagination!!! I praise God for His great and wondrous love.

I am sure Jebastin was praying and longing for a mother's love. As the word of God says, "*Delight yourself in the Lord and I will give you the desire of your heart.*" Psalm 37:4 And that is exactly what happened in his life.

And with Sister Amy, it was similar. She wanted a child and God honored her prayers, gifting her with a "ready-made" child – a missing piece in her life. I saw how Jebastin grew closer to his mom during our short stay. He got so close that he would not allow anyone else to sit near his mom!!! He would always stick to his mother and to his grandma Jo-Ann too!!!

When it was time for Sister Amy and her mom's departure, Jebastin was deeply saddened and became emotional. He did not want them to go. It was heartbreaking to see them parting from each other. I pray that God will bring them back together very soon. I believe Jebastin has treasured a mother's and grandma's love in his heart that he will never forget though they are far away from each other. I pray he will always feel the warmth of his mother's love. Amen!!!!

♥ ♥ ♥

Kanagaveli Ragael, Jebastin's grandmother

Because my daughter, Jebastin's mother, was sick, I took her youngest son Abishek into my home as an infant. He was just three days old. My daughter died a short time later. I visited her in the hospital, and she asked for some coffee. It was almost midnight, but I got the coffee for her anyway. As we were drinking the coffee together, she asked me to take care of her children. Then she called out the name of Jesus and died. And then Angel and Jebastin also came to stay with me. Jebastin was five, and his sister, Angel, was seven years.

A few years later, my husband died, and life was very difficult. Somehow God provided. Many times, I did not eat so the children could eat. I struggled to care for three children because I had a very small income.

When Jebastin got a sponsor through Compassion International, I was very happy. My expenses were reduced, and it became easier to care for all three children. His school fees, tuition, and other educational supplies were covered. I thanked God every day for Amy, his sponsor. I prayed for her and her family, even after Compassion closed.

Because of the Compassion program, Jebastin had joy in his life. I could truly tell a difference. He was happier than Angel and Abishek because he participated in field trips and tours with compassion. He also had spiritual instruction and learned about Jesus. Up until he was in about 9th grade, he was very involved in church activities.

The summer after his 12th grade year, he went to VBS classes in our church. After three days of VBS he was in a major bike accident. I know God protected him from death. After that I noticed he was avoiding the church. He was out roaming with friends. But later his faith in Jesus grew stronger and he followed him again. The seeds that had been planted in his life came to bear fruit after all.

♥ ♥ ♥

Lavanya, Jebastin's fiancée

I have known Jebastin since 2012. We met because I visited his home with a friend, who is Jebastin's cousin. He proposed to me on February 1, 2014 and we started doing everything together. I love him so much, but there were some problems along the way. He began doing some crazy things, and he would become angry and shout even for small problems in life.

A few years later, I learned that Jebastin was using drugs. I told him to leave that kind of life, but he did not. He lied to me and said he would stop, but I knew he had not stopped. One day we met up at the beach. I was angry with him because he told me that he was going to stop using drugs, but I found he was still using them that day. I took it from him and threw it away.

One day, months later, he came to talk with me. He said, "I have surrendered myself to God." I was wondering if it were true. I had asked him for many years, but he did not do it. But now how was it possible? Then I realized God heard my prayers. I prayed every day, but he did not surrender himself to Jesus.

When Jebastin's sponsor Amy visited India, only then did I realize: It was not only my prayer for Jebastin that God heard. His American Mom and Grandma and many other people were also praying for him. And so, he changed because God heard the prayers of everyone. I am very happy about that.

Now, instead of spending time with the wrong friends, he is always in church. Last Christmas Jebastin wrote the script for the church youth group. I love to see how God is using Jebastin's life!

♥ ♥ ♥

Jerald, Jebastin's cousin

Good seeds were planted in Jebastin's life by his sponsor, Amy. But for several years, he didn't live in righteousness and he was very rude with everyone. This was after his 12th grade year.

I had surrendered my life to Jesus in 2015 during my church camp. After that I thought about my family and my cousins who were born into a Christian family but were not true Christians in their hearts. I invited all my cousins to church and other activities. One day in my prayer time, God spoke to me about talking with Jebastin.

I invited him to church many times, but he did not come. He avoided me. I kept praying for him. For 2 to 3 months, every Sunday morning I would go and invite him to come to church. I knew he was doing bad things, but then one day he came with me to church.

That day he accepted Jesus as the Savior of his life again. After that, things went well, but sometimes he was suffering. He was very angry and would hit himself or break things. But God helped him come out of that.

When he found Amy on Facebook, he told everyone in our family; He was so excited! After he connected with her again, I saw many good changes in his life. He read the

Bible in three months. He started praying and having devotions every day. He started going to the prayer meetings and church. God used Amy in Jebastin's life, and I am thankful that God used me to play a part, too.

♥ ♥ ♥

Angel, Jebastin's sister

My brother, Jebastin, was always in my home. I knew he felt alone in his younger days because he isolated himself from everyone. He was jealous of me and our brother Abishek, but he did not spend time with us. After days out running around, he talked with me, and we became friends. Even then, he still felt alone. He would always sit alone on our terrace. After his 12th grade year was over, I found out he was using drugs. This made me very sad, but I did not tell our Grandma. I did not want her to send him out of the home. What would he do then?

Before his 12th grade he was always in church. He regularly went to compassion. He had a few friends near my home, and he would always sit and talk with them. But after 12th grade he spoiled his life, and I was very worried about him. He had started using drugs to get high, and then his character changed. He was always very rude to others. He even stopped sharing anything with me about his sorrow. Instead, he was suffering alone and turned to drugs.

But now, everything has changed. He has turned his life back over to God. I think God used Amy, his sponsor, in his life in an amazing way. Because of the seeds his sponsor planted in his life, Jebastin is now following Christ and serving others.

♥ ♥ ♥

Suresh, Jebastin's friend

I have known Jebastin since primary school. We were close friends and spent a lot of time together. When my father died, I left the school to help my mother and brother. Without my father, she needed my help. Sometimes I saw Jebastin around town. After I left school, he changed to a school for grades 11 and 12. During that time, I did not see him, but we stayed in touch. I had his landline number. Sometimes when I was free, I would call him and talk. I saw him around 2015 and his life was very different. He had changed and was using drugs. Sometimes he would even call me to invite me to use drugs, too. I did not do it.

After a few years, I met him again. He had totally changed again. He shared the Gospel with me. I was shocked how his life had changed like this. I thought he might be just acting, but after time, I could see that he truly had changed. When I met his sponsor, Amy, and saw how she impacted his life. That's when I realized God heard all the prayers she prayed for Jebastin. My life has also been impacted, and I am changed.

♥♥♥

Karthick, Jebastin's friend

I have known Jebastin since we were in 9th grade. At that time, I did not get along with him. We always fought with each other because we were in competition over our class teacher Sarah. We became friends during our 11th grade year. But I did not know him well and after we finished school, we did not see each other until 2015. At that time, we became good friends with a strong bond. A little while later, I could tell that Jebastin had a drug problem. Many times, I told him to be careful and get out of that life, but he did not listen to me. I saw there was sadness in his heart, but I did not know why, and I did not ask him.

Jebastin was defending Christianity even if he was doing wrong things himself. I was wondering why he was like this. Then, one day he came to visit me and told me that he had decided to live for Jesus. I was surprised by his seemingly sudden decision. But I noticed a change in his life. He talked about the Bible every day, and at lunchtime he played Christian songs. He kept asking me to come to church with him. One time, I finally went to the youth fellowship with him. I realized then that he was not acting, and he was sincere. He encouraged me many times to study the Bible.

In early 2018, we were working in the office around 3 pm. Jebastin suddenly jumped up and kissed me! I did not understand and thought he was acting or overreacting. He said he had found Amy on Facebook. I knew about his sponsor, and he had told me about the birthday gifts he received, and he always said that his sponsor was the reason he played football (soccer) and believed in Jesus and studied hard in school.

In 2020, when Amy came to Chennai to visit, that was when truly I realized just how much he was impacted by her. Jebastin always told me, "God has a plan for everything." In Jebastin's life, I can see God's plan. I can see how Jebastin served God, and God took care of his needs. I also feel blessed to have the chance to meet Amy and Jo-Ann and Sarah during their visit. I am glad it was part of the plan!

♥ ♥ ♥

Pause to Ponder

Who are the people in your life that represent your great cloud of witnesses?

What do you hope they notice about your walk with God?

What do you think they would say they have learned from you?

♥ ♥ ♥

Noteworthy Notes

Helpful Resources

Helpful Resources

The Romans Road

First and foremost, we share our story for God's glory. Our personal relationship with Jesus has made all the difference in our lives. If you do not already know Jesus as your personal Savior, we hope you are inspired to learn more, and take action to accept him.

You may send either of us a private message to ask questions. We would be honored to answer any questions you have. To explore on your own, take the "Romans Road:"

The Problem	Romans 3:23
	Romans 3:10
The Consequences	Romans 5:12
	Romans 6:23
The Scope	Romans 1:20
The Response	Romans 10:9-10
The Assurance	Romans 10:13
The Result	Romans 5:1
	Romans 8:1
	Romans 8:38-39

Business & Nonprofit Links

Our business interests and colleagues have been an important part of our journeys. Below is a list of various businesses or nonprofits that have supported our growth along the way. These organizations offer hope and assistance to others. If you have interest in learning more, you may contact one of us, or use the websites or email addresses listed below to find more information.

Ambassador Advisors	www.ambassadoradvisors.com/
Celebrate Recovery	www.celebraterecovery.com
Christian Missions Charitable Trust	https://cmctindia.in/
Compassion International	www.compassion.com
Eastern Mennonite Missions	www.emm.org
Hope Family Trust	http://www.hopefamilytrusts.org/
Jeevan Dataa Ministries	jeevandataministries@yahoo.co.in
The John Maxwell Team	www.yourjmtpc.com
Young Living Essential Oils	https://getoiling.com/amyjmalay
Youth With a Mission	www.ywam.org

Child Abuse Awareness

As a person who experienced childhood abuse, Amy wants to raise awareness for children all over the world who are suffering "under the radar" due to the lack of awareness. Please look up the link below to read more about the statistics of child abuse. You can make a difference for children by raising your awareness.

https://arkofhopeforchildren.org/child-abuse/child-abuse-statistics-info

Willing to Share

We would love the opportunity to share our story in person or virtually! For information about having one or both of us share a message of hope and encouragement with your group, send an email to:

amyjmalay@gmail.com or jebastinbenny2@gmail.com.

Amy is an experienced international speaker and coach, certified by The John Maxwell Team. Proceeds from her speaking and coaching work benefit local and international nonprofits. She delights in serving adults or youth in person or virtually with individual coaching, group coaching, workshops, and assessments. Topics include:

- Personal & Spiritual Growth
- Transformed Mindset
- Parenting & Family
- DISC Personality System
- Leadership | The Leadership Game
- Communication & Connection
- Sales & Networking
- John Maxwell Academy Online Courses
- Chemical Free Living with Essential Oils
- Wellness with Essential Oils
- Aroma Freedom with Essential Oils

https://www.johncmaxwellgroup.com/amyjmalay/

♥ ♥ ♥

#HeNeverStopsWorking

♥ ♥ ♥

Noteworthy Notes

♥ ♥ ♥